Paddle Beads

Paddle Beads

O. Ross McIntyre

Illustrations by Bert Dodson

GRAYBOOKS
LYME, NEW HAMPSHIRE

ISBN-10: 1-935655-12-4
ISBN-13: 978-1-935655-12-1
Library of Congress Catalog Number: 2010931811

Published by
GrayBooks LLC
1 Main Street
Lyme, New Hampshire 03768
www.GraybooksPublishers.com

Paperback Edition

Printed in The Unites States of America
on acid-free paper.

For Jean

Contents

Preface

JUST UP THE CONNECTICUT RIVER from where I live in New Hampshire the river makes a sharp bend to the east and heads toward Mt. Moosilauke, 15 miles away. At this bend a picturesque red barn is posed against the distant view of this fine mountain. On a blue-sky day, the barn makes an excellent subject for a photo. If you go ashore and step out of your canoe on that bend you will find yourself standing in the overlapping footprints of the many photographers who have stood, all in the same spot, to record this scene.

It is probably because of a life spent as a physician, researcher and teacher that I find the presence of the overlapping footprints amusing. Advances in medical knowledge depend upon the researcher challenging conventional wisdom and viewing a problem from a new perspective. Innovation in medicine and patient care arises from the same roots as innovation in the arts. Here we recognize creativity as success in portraying the world as seen from new viewpoints. So as I start this book I ask the question: Is there some way that those who travel these pages can encounter images that are different from those in other books about canoeing?

As you will learn here, in my many years of paddling on the rivers and lakes of this globe my background in biology and medicine has caused me to record things that others on the same routes may have missed. You will not find descriptions of new canoe routes and new lands here. I have tried to paddle in some places that may never have seen a canoe before but these are not places I like to remember or talk about. And the world does not really need another book about familiar lakes and rivers written by someone standing in exactly the same footprints of the real explorers.

Much of this book is based upon notes scribbled into the waterproof spiral-bound surveyor's notebooks that have traveled in my shirt pocket on river, lake, and ocean. These notes record what I saw and felt on those days. I believe they also tell me something about how I became the person I am today.

It is not a guidebook, or a how-to-do book although there are bits of both in it. Although one trip is described in some detail, I am deliberately vague about where some of the other events described here occurred.

For years, my wife Jean and I planned our yearly canoe trip with care and approached our departure with joy and high spirits. Some people wonder how a physician who cares for cancer patients can perform this work without becoming depressed. Caring for those with cancer is a demanding occupation and important discoveries in cancer treatment come only after a lot of hard work. The physician's reward comes from the increasing number of cancer patients who are cured each year. And for me there was an added reward: each year I could refill the well holding my doses of compassion by heading for some remote territory where I could paddle.

After my retirement, Jean and I realized that there was no law against going on more than one trip a year. In each of the years following this wonderful discovery we paddled 500 to 1,000 miles until Jean's illness intervened. Even after her bone marrow transplant, however, we paddled the Okefenokee and picked mussels for our dinner from seaside rocks in the Hebrides.

For those of you whose hands have not yet grown a paddle callus I hope I offer a glimpse of what you will encounter as your paddle becomes a real companion. For those with miles of water behind you and more to come, I trust that these pieces will offer insights on why we pack our canoes so carefully and why we enjoy the sensation as the bow rises on a wave or as we lean the canoe into a turn. And for those who are content to sit comfortably at the fireside and dream about the way things should be, may the book give your imagination something to chew on.

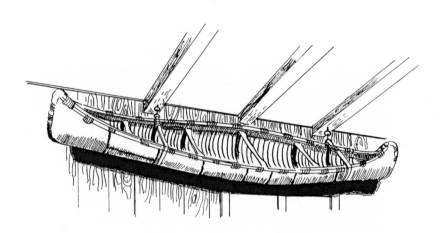

Engle

"DON'T LET THE CANVAS OF YOUR CANOE or the wood of the paddle touch anything but air or water. I don't ever want to hear noise from the paddle or the canoe. Remember, air or water!"

Engle sat next to the canoe shed, the brim of his peaked felt hat close to his eyebrows, scanning the water, watching. This was a test I had to pass before I could go to Canada and into the Quetico. It was 1945 and I was 13 years old. Engle sent me out in a red cedar and canvas canoe, the subject of a recent restoration in his careful hands—sent me downwind toward the distant stony point, where I was to turn the canoe around and return. He knew that I wouldn't be able to turn the canoe when I got it there.

I began my turn well before the point, but as I brought the canoe through the first part of the turn, the wind coming from astern caught the bow and the turn ended at 90 degrees. I struggled, trying again and again, but didn't have the strength to complete the turn. I prayed for the wind to stop, and looked up the lake to Engle who remained sitting, regular puffs of smoke emerging from his pipe as he assessed my repeated failures. At last the wind pushed me upon the rocky point and I violated his rule about paddles and canvas. As I stepped out of the boat into the sloshing water and turned the canoe around before it was bashed, I noted that Engle was now standing and looking even more grim than usual.

Returning upwind, I let the wind whip the bow of the canoe into the opening between the two canoe docks, grasped a dock to prevent the boat from bumping, and steadied it in the water. Engle was there above me, pipe now held in one hand while he held the bow of my canoe with the other. He then quietly told me how to turn a canoe around in the wind—a lesson I would never forget.

I set out again. This time I was kneeling near the center of the canoe. As I approached the point I began my turn, crawling forward so that the bow was now lower in the water than the stern. My former enemy, the wind, did the turning, pushing the stern in an arc around the bow and I was headed back toward the gray face under the pointed hat. There was no celebration. It would not have been tolerated, but Engle and I had bonded: teacher and student.

I met Engle, a high school teacher of German extraction at Camp Vermilion, a boy's camp in northern Minnesota. As he supervised activities in the craft-house or in the canoe shed the sharp features of his gray face instilled discipline in otherwise casual youths. His grip on the steering wheel of his 1936 Ford Sedan was as secure as his control of the young campers that were crammed into the back seat. There was no nonsense among us as the car sped over remote gravel roads.

Most successful enterprises have a guy like Engle somewhere in their structure. The camp director, Dubendorf, an outgoing enthusiast for the summer camp experience, had enough sense not to send Engle on the winter trips that sold the value of camp to parents in various midwestern cities. He would have flopped in public relations. However, when the "one lunger" gas engine that pumped lake water to the camp water tower failed, it was Engle who got it going again, and it was Engle's car that pulled the trailer loaded with packs and canoes. These talents were not lost on boys who recognized competence when it appeared before them. While our homebound parents during those World War II years planned their meals only after counting their meat ration coupons, Engle shot and dressed the bear we campers ate at a memorable dinner.

On our way to Crane Lake up on the Canadian border, Engle's overloaded Ford skittered on the washboard and its rear end was pushed sideways by the pole of the heavily laden canoe trailer until the whole rig landed in the ditch. He was unfazed. While young boys kicked at the impressive newly hatched ruts and wondered where a tow truck could be found in this semi wilderness, Engle unhitched the trailer. Directing where we should place our effort, he had us push the trailer back and then with lots of coordination but little work we lifted and pushed the Ford from the ditch.

In addition to learning about canoe turns I learned something else at Camp Vermilion. Each morning the campers rose early to reveille and were in their bunks again by taps at night. One camper had his bill reduced in return for his services with the bugle—for getting up 5 minutes early and going to bed 5 minutes later than the rest of us. In the same sense that the local TV weatherman may project authority and achieve celebrity by telling us what the weather will be, the bugler gained status by, in effect, making us get up or lie down. His job was made harder by our frequent attempts to hide his bugle, or failing that, to surreptitiously fill it with water so that the first note of reveille was a gargle.

During that memorable summer, the camp bugler became hooked, too. Not on the concept of gliding a canoe through pristine waters but rather on his desires for the beautiful daughter of one of the counselors. This girl and her mother lived as in a convent, their small cabin well out of the mainstream of camp traffic. Although the rest of the campers sometimes spotted an attractive girl visiting the camp kitchen, none of us had connected her either to the counselor or to the cabin. Some young men, however, are blessed with uncanny powers of deduction derived from the hormone switch, and the bugler had soon connected the dots that defined this particular relationship. Infatuation clouds judgment and the ability to keep secrets. Soon, an expanding circle of campers was aware of his desires and found joy in teasing him about his fantasies.

One day, perhaps agitated by our teasing, the bugler made the mistake of expressing his desires explicitly and loudly enough for the father of the girl to hear them. The counselor immediately complained to the camp director. I was astounded by what happened.

While we campers regarded the bugler's goals as idle boasts—as kidding around—this was not the view of the director. The director's smooth public interface covered a steel infrastructure, that was, I suspect, hardened by Engle's tactical support. The result was a punishment that made us all take notice.

The usual punishment in camp was a "red owl," delivered by the assembled campers formed into a gantlet through which the offender ran. With speed and some agility it was possible to avoid a few of the intended lashes from the campers' leather belts, but it was painful. Sometimes, multiple red owls were awarded for serious infractions. This was what we expected for the bugler.

We were wrong. His punishment came quietly. He was removed from the day-to-day routines of the camp and met for extended periods with the camp leaders. We whispered to each other about what these sessions might be like for the bugler. I suppose today we might call what went on as "counseling." This approach made it clear to the campers that Dubendorf and Engle regarded the bugler's expressed wish as far more threatening than the offenses that generated red owls.

In shame, the bugler served his sentence while the young campers learned their lesson; men we respected found that such talk was unacceptable. In so doing, they offered us an inkling of an idea that most of us had never encountered before. An idea that made us ask who that young woman really was, and what she was really like. They told us young men that she deserved our respect.

Years later, I became upset as I watched our women hospital employees walk to work from the parking lot past a construction site surrounded by bricklayer's scaffolding. Protected by distance and the cover of blowing tarps, the laborers launched dozens of catcalls, whistles and rude remarks that rained down upon these women. It would have been wonderful to have Dubendorf and Engle step out onto that scaffolding to put an end to it. In retrospect, my Camp Vermilion lesson in manners was at least as important to me as learning how to turn a canoe on a windy day.

Forty years later, I canoed down Lake Vermilion again. I paddled past the point where I had received my wind-paddling lesson and landed on the shore where the craft house and canoe shed had once stood. Much of the lakeside property had been sold and new vacation homes replaced the once familiar paths and clumps of alder. Leaving the canoe and walking up the hill I found parts of the old camp, now used as a retreat by the church that had bought the property. The cabin I had stayed in was still there as was the dining hall, the largest structure in the camp. I wondered whether there was still a birch bark canoe hanging from the ceiling of that large hall—a scene that Dubendorf and Engle had planned for all of us.

They may have known that the soft brown of the inner bark, now forming the outer surface of the hull, the lacing of spruce roots, the black of spruce gum would cast its spell on at least a few of the youths who ate under it. In my case our leaders had cast well. I learned that something beautiful and functional could be created from what was found around us. My young horizon was stretched.

So it was that I came to understand the beauty of the shape and substance of a canoe; how it is to fashion simple things into a boat that could carry my packs and glide through the water leaving only a ripple, a craft that would set me free in nature unapproachable by any other means. It was at this camp, on the water and in the dining hall that my love affair with canoes became serious, and since then I have been hooked.

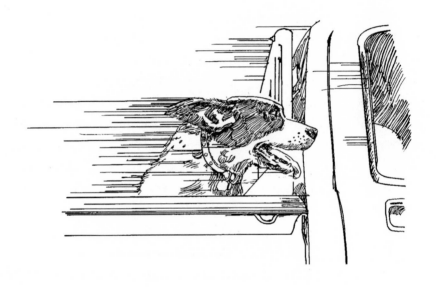

Why Do They Spin?

THERE IS NO HAPPINESS LIKE THE DOG with its head out the window of a fast moving car, unless it is the dog in the back of a pickup with his head curled around into the air stream. Thirty-five years ago one local dog often rode unrestrained on the fabric roof of a Model A pickup and to my knowledge never fell off. (Though I will admit that this particular pickup never had the upgrade to hydraulic brakes). I thought that concern over eye protection and the introduction of metal roofs had eliminated this mode of riding, but just a few days ago I spotted a delightful pooch, legs widespread on a shiny steel roof within the tentative enclosure of a ladder rack, while the pickup leaned outward in a sharp corner. Dogs smile and this one was smiling.

Motion gratifies. For this reason snowmobiles and water skiers circle; sleds, skis and toboggans slide; sport planes fly low; and bored suburbanites take several trips to the mall per day despite the lack of any real need to do so. As children we are rocked to sleep, and as seniors we swing gently on the porch glider. The Shelburne Museum in Vermont has preserved a couple of adult-sized cradles that were at one time employed to gently rock aged invalids into their passing. Give me such a way out—a rocker energized by a child's or grandchild's foot while they hum a favorite tune.

There is motion from our very beginning. In the cushion of amniotic fluid we turn and kick, unrestrained by our flexible lifeline to the placenta. When this arrangement is abruptly terminated it makes us unhappy enough to cry—our nine-month swim has ended on a cold and unyielding beach. Later, in a warm blanket and held against a shoulder, our night cries vanish in gentle motion as our parents walk us. We are reminded again of the security that so comforted us during our fluid phase.

Lots of animals spend their entire lives swimming around in fluid. Our own embryonic heritage traces to creatures of the sea. The shark's positioning device of three semicircular canals is retained almost without change in our mammalian skull. The gentle rocking motion of the sea comforts us; the violent agitation of it in a storm frightens us. For us, the discontinuity—where the motion of water meets the stability of the land—is where the opportunities and the risks lie. It is from here we venture forth on the land to the realities of travel with fixed waypoints, or onto the water where things are never fixed, where waypoints must be inferred, and motion never ceases.

Children can't get enough of motion. Sometimes they spin in circles in the middle of the room in order to get dizzy, aggravating their parents when they bunch the rug or fall into the lamps. Soon they crash to the floor where they lie with the room still spinning. Though it may be somewhat uncomfortable, lying there while the room and its contents whiz by, it is not truly noxious. If so, they wouldn't spin again just a few minutes later. They do it for the unique sensations it generates. "Hey, I'm dizzy!"

The figure skater begins a spin with the arms outstretched. Moving them closer to the body, the energy stored in those outstretched arms is converted to spin, and his body becomes a blur of rapid rotation. Why doesn't the skater crash to the ice like the child spinning on the rug? Notice how the skater's head moves. Coaches teach skaters when spinning to fix their eyes on one object and to ignore the rest that spin past. On each rotation the skater's head snaps to a fixed position for just an instant, and then catches up with the rotation. During that instant, the skater's eyes see just what they saw when the head snapped into position the last trip around. The body spins; what the eye sees does not.

So the eye as well as the ear tells us which way is up. One cold moonless night a few years ago, with the overcast eliminating starlight, some old college buddies and I skied down an easy trail at the Dartmouth Skiway. By using our peripheral vision we could see enough trees to get some sense as to the whereabouts of the edges of the trail. We went slowly, weighted down by our backpacks, and gaining whatever clues we could from the behavior of our skis. The interesting feature of this trip was not that we fell down while moving, but rather that we fell when we came to a stop. The stopping set the fluid in our semicircular canals into motion and without clues from the eyes to tell us we were stopped, caused our balance mechanisms to throw us onto the ground. Even when we had figured out what was causing us to fall, the vestibular signals were so strong that we could not use intellect to overpower them.

Looking out of the window of a moving train, our eyes fix on an object of interest and slowly follow it as it falls behind. When it is no longer comfortable to view that object, our eyes snap rapidly in the direction of travel and fix on something new. Look at your fellow passenger's reflection in the window, and observe the repeated slow and fast eye movements. Then look at the eyes of the spinning children who have just crashed to the rug. Their eyes will move slowly away from the direction of their rotation and then snap back in the direction of rotation. There is a name for this eye motion: "nystagmus." The cop who is investigating an accident rousts the college student whose car displays fresh dings and who is sleeping with his foot on the floor. He focuses his flashlight on the student's eyes. Aha! Nystagmus. Time to do the rest of the sobriety tests and to measure an alcohol level.

From my canoe I watch the passing bank, putting the distant reach of river or next bend into my peripheral vision. Like the train passenger, my eyes fix on some object on the riverbank and examine it until my body is carried past the point of convenient inspection and my eyes snap forward to fix on another object of interest. At other times, my sight is directed at a distant point down river. The riverbank passes, blurred as it goes out of my field of vision on the right and left sides. That distant point of focus creeps ahead as the banks glide by. I move along in an un-roofed tunnel of passing trees and steep valley walls.

Focused on the down-river view and pleased by the sense of motion I easily miss the minimal clues that "dead man's rock" provides. I may miss seeing the stone sheep high on the canyon wall. A tumbled cabin passes silently in woods beyond my peripheral vision. A mile after the entrance of a tributary I notice the laminar flow of its colored water at the edge of the stream. A fine black bear comes out on a ledge a few feet away and dips his mouth for a drink, but goes unseen.

If, instead of looking downstream, my eyes are fixed on the river-bank, I am constantly surprised by tricks the river plays. I get hung up frequently in channels that lack water and am late to see the sweeper in the upcoming bend. I'm unable to say whether the stream coming in from the side is a tributary or simply the rejoining of the river after an island.

While we travel, most of us cycle between these two views, one the riverbank and the other, the view downstream. Our eyes shift direction, automatically adjusting the focus to near or to far as required. From our semicircular canals come other signals of what we are up to, a rise and fall with a wave, a spin into an eddy. Putting these signals together, we are alert to the world around us, in touch with what is going on. We scan.

The airlines have long recognized that some pilots "scan" efficiently and that others have trouble doing so. Scanning in this connection refers to a systematic viewing of the instruments, controls and attitude of the plane that in good pilots has become automatic. Scanning can be taught but some pilots never acquire this skill. They get washed out of airline training, and I hope I never encounter such a failure in a float plane. Most canoeists scan just fine. If you recognize yourself as a person who is fixed on only one view of the river, if you are the person who never sees the bear, you are a person who cannot scan. Take some friends along.

But why does the child spin? I suggest that when eye motions and the signals from our semicircular canals occur at levels our minds recognize as non-threatening, we recognize them as pleasurable sensations. Looking from the train window or from the canoe to the bank signals the primitive portions of our brain to make us content. To be fully effective in generating this mood, our position in space as defined by what we see and what our semicircular canals are telling us must agree. When the two disagree, we are frightened.

And why should eye movements and those of the ear canals make us happy? Because motion and travel is important for our survival as a species. By travel we gain knowledge of our surroundings. This has survival benefits: tactical advantage over our enemies, discovery of food sources, location of improved shelter. The more we travel and the more people we encounter, the more likely we are to find attractive mates thereby diversifying the human gene pool.

When asked to explain why they canoe, many canoeists will offer an explanation based upon the discovery of natural wonders: spectacular water, views of virgin territory, encounters with exotic wildlife. Some try to gain bragging points by describing trips of daunting hardship and privation and others relate the benefits of a temporary withdrawal from a complex urban society. All of these play some role in the decision to take a canoe trip. But beneath all these explanations I believe is a common factor. As the canoeist coasts along, wafted by the current, an occasional flick of the paddle to straighten the canoe's path, the boat carries a load that would break a backpacker. The scenery streams past, the paddler's eyes fix on fireweed in bloom, or on the smooth mud of an otter slide. The eyes follow it as it passes upstream. Then the eyes snap forward to the next object of interest. From deep within the primitive part of the paddler's brain the call goes out, "Attention! Attention! You are feeling good!"

Why Do They Spin?

Rock Prints

THE CREASE IN THE ALUMINUM began just ahead of the first rib, about where the bowperson's foot rested. It continued for 20 inches toward the stern in a pattern suggesting a sketched lightning bolt. The first rib had been pried up a bit by the impact—a solid hit, but the canoe was still structurally sound. There were no leaks. It was a 17 foot Grumman square stern and Jack Wright who owned it had just passed his 65th birthday. The square sterns were made by cutting a foot off an 18 footer and adding a small transom, extra ribs, spray rails, and a large rear seat containing flotation. They are not a lightweight boat. Jack found the job of lifting it onto his car harder each year and had just purchased a nice light Kevlar replacement.

Although the canoe was rated for a three horsepower motor, Jack had a Johnson 5.5 horsepower outboard on it. Revved up and with a rock counterweight holding the bow down, it would plane. He was going slower than that when he hit the crease-making rock an hour's floatplane ride north of Chibougamau. Jack was one of a group from my medical center that traveled to the far north for serious fishing. Once a year, they would return from their trip with stories of huge lake trout, and proudly show off the newly broken windshield of their car—thanks to the passing ore trucks and flying gravel on the northern roads.

I wondered whether I would ever be able to travel those northern lands. Jack and his group were senior faculty physicians and I had just arrived in the Medical Center as a young recruit. Although I dreamed of traveling northern rivers, for the moment my young family needed a canoe to cross a small pond to a cottage that lacked road access on the far shore. Jack's price for the canoe and motor was less than I had expected to pay for the canoe alone. Our deal was soon made and I purchased our first canoe.

While bystanders commented that our canoe was missing its stern, Jean and I loaded three children, the dog, and food for the weekend into our trustworthy craft and paddled it across the pond to the cottage. Those were wonderful times. We had saved enough to buy a new budget-priced 1967 Chevrolet and had already placed the order when Jean and the children spotted the classified ad for the cottage. The car and the cottage cost the same, $3,500, and deciding which would give more pleasure to three children and Jean took less than a moment. Our two oldest, Jeanie and Ross, age 8 and 6, (tradition demanded that their first name match that of their parents), and Elizabeth, 2, loved the idea of a place on the water and so we bought it. The joy we found there offset the tribulation of maintaining our second-hand Oldsmobile and living with its cantaloupe-sized rust holes in the trunk for two more years until we could afford something better.

Our children learned to paddle. They swam with the boat, swamping it, pushing it down until it rose like a whale sounding. It moved 100 pound propane cylinders, 2-by-4s and 4-by-8-foot sheets of plywood. It carried distinguished visitors or broken bedsprings with equal ease. It set us free on the water, as does any canoe, but this was one that required no care or maintenance.

Then in November of 1973 I went to bring it in for the winter. When I reached the shoreline tree where it had been chained it was gone! Its chain, padlock still attached, was there, shiny in the place where the bolt cutters had sliced through it. Now for the first time in my life, I realized how an otherwise normal person could murder. If I had come upon the person cutting that chain, I might have done my best to kill him. I reported the theft to the police who expressed little hope of its recovery while Jean, the kids and I went into mourning over our loss.

I found a new 18 foot Grumman to replace it, and on Christmas Day Jeanie and Elizabeth pretended to paddle it out of the barn through the snow while Ross, hidden within the doorway, provided motive force to the snowy scene. Jean was completely surprised. The Christmas present meant that we once more were free to travel by canoe, but the new one lacked seven years of happy memories. We never bonded to it as to our old friend that lacked the last foot of hull.

Ten more years passed. We bought other canoes and paddled them on northern rivers. One day, as Jean and I prepared to set off on such a trip, I spotted an ad in the newspaper. "Grumman square stern canoe, 17 feet, good condition, $350." A local phone number was listed. Putting off our departure on the trip for a bit, I went to have a look at the canoe. It was red, a poorly done paint job, faded from years of sun and weather exposure. The oval plaque bearing the Grumman logo was missing, rivets snapped off. I looked at the hull near the bow. There it was: a crease beginning at the point where the bow person's foot rested, continuing to the rear in a pattern resembling sketched lightning. The first rib was distorted, surely raised by the encounter with that rock north of Chibougamau. Rock prints like this one must identify an aluminum canoe as reliably as fingerprints identify a person.

I looked at the man who was selling. We didn't make satisfactory eye contact. He said he was moving away from the area and that he was selling the canoe so that it wouldn't have to be moved. I knew the family had been in several scrapes with the authorities.

"How long have you had the canoe?"

"Oh, I dunno, maybe three years."

"Where did you get it?"

"From a guy in Longmeadow, Massachusetts." he said, eye contact further than ever.

I thought about explaining creases in aluminum to a judge who had never paddled a canoe. Could I succeed?

The signs of the seller's impending departure—rental moving equipment and boxes—were lying about. Jean and I needed to get going—to head north into Canada and our river trip. So I sighed, wrote out a check and we bought our own canoe back.

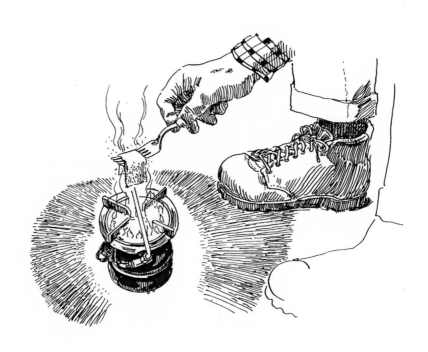

The Williams Creek Mining Co.

THE FIRE HAD JUMPED THE YUKON and now both sides of the river were blackened. Despite the rain, a number of glowing hot spots remained, spewing out the eye-stinging smoke of burning spruce. In that mess campsites were going to be hard to find.

Far ahead on river left Jean and I could see a swatch of unburned forest ascending a hill. Where the slope ended in a cut-bank that dropped to the river a couple of people in colorful raingear appeared near the beach. Seconds later several canoes came into view, drawn up on the gravel where Williams Creek entered the Yukon. The current was swift and soon we were there.

"Any room for us to camp up there?"

"Yes, come on up."

We unwrapped the skirts that tied us into the spray cover on the canoe. As we did so we could feel heat from the warm "basement" beneath the cover dissipate into the cold rain. By now we could see what the two women were up to. They had carved an oven in the face of the sandy bank and were trying to get a fire going in it. The wood was wet, the rain continued to pour down on their wood pile and they had not built a flue to provide a draft for their oven. Lots of smoke, little fire.

"Pizza, tonight," one of them shouted to us as we started to unload the boat. She had an accent, German, maybe Swiss, I thought.

We lugged our gear to the top of the bank, where we could see a couple of derelict buildings on a bit of level ground. A painted board sign announced, "Williams Creek Mining Co." Smoke issued from between the loose boards and gable end of the larger building. From the looks of it, the building had served as a machine shop for the mine operation. Inside a fire was burning on the dirt floor, the smoke rising into the loft. Around the fire was a group trying to get dinner together.

Jean and I climbed the hill above the buildings. We passed by several tents on our way up and soon found a rounded knob of smooth ground occupied by a few medium sized and conveniently spaced birches. We had a view across the river. To the north a good sized hill, a partner to the one we were on, created a narrow spot in the valley. This hill disappeared into a mix of clouds and smoke about 200 feet above the river. To the south the land was flatter but obscured by patches of fog and smoke.

By the time we had carried our gear to this spot, the rain had let up and within minutes we had our tent up. Soon we had a tarp over it. The tarp covered enough additional space to create a dry "front porch" with a view of the Yukon and the hills. With both doors of the tent wide open the soft breeze began to ventilate the tent that was still damp from the night before. To get it fully dry would require some body heat, however. By now the rain had started again.

We broke off some dead branches for firewood and went down the hill to the tumble-down building. The two young women who had been working on the pizza oven were now inside. They were Swiss and were guiding a party of about 10. Their oven fire never burned well and the sandy roof of the oven had collapsed on what little fire they had. The pizza dough was going to be fried not baked.

Nearly everyone spoke English. They had started at the ghost town of Dyea, the head of the Chilkoot Trail near Skagway, Alaska and had taken the route of many of those who participated in the Klondike gold rush of 1898. After climbing Chilkoot pass they descended to Bennett Lake where they had then loaded their packs into canoes awaiting them there. After traversing the big lakes at the head of the Yukon they then paddled past Whitehorse and were on their way to Dawson City. It had been a rough trip for them. Chilkoot pass is steep, and it is a long way from Dawson City. On the river they first had to endure smoke and fire, and later steady rain.

We had started on the Teslin River at Johnson Crossing and met the Yukon at the abandoned police outpost at Hootalinga, thereby avoiding the foot blisters of the Chilkoot. We also had better gear to cope with the weather. They had sought this ramshackle shelter as their best option after another day of rain. Although the roof leaked badly, it shed at least a fraction of the rain. What water came through the roof then hit a ceiling composed of tongue and groove boards. Holding the broken boards together was a layer of dirty canvas. Since this ceiling did little to divert the leaks, the party had rigged a large tarp under the canvas. It was necessary to push up on the tarp from time to time to discharge the heavy loads of water that pooled within it. Laughter and warnings in a mix of languages announced the impending deluge of tarp water.

They invited us to join them, and although it would have been drier for us to cook under our tarp, we climbed the hill, got our food and stove, and returned with more firewood. With hot food and drink, plus a variety of spirits, the crowd began to feel happier. About this time, a fellow came over to Jean and me. He was probably in his 40s, a big guy. There was something about his approach that suggested confrontation rather than socialization.

"I'm leaving this trip tomorrow. Can't stand it anymore."

"Where? How?"

"At Little Salmon. The map shows a jeep trail to the highway." His gestures were a little coarse, his eyes darted a bit, but he could provide answers to our questions.

"Have you told your guides?' Neither of us was making any effort to avoid being overheard.

"I will tomorrow at Little Salmon. I can't take it!"

"It is a long walk. There may be no one at Little Salmon." I suspected that the guides had already heard him describe his plans several times.

"I can't take it anymore."

Then we noticed a person we had overlooked. He sat off to one side, scrunched down along the sill of the building, knees drawn up, and staring straight ahead. His expression was absolutely flat. Nothing that anyone said to him or did near him produced a reaction. Catatonic.

"Good God," I thought. Here we have two young women leading a trip that includes one guy who is probably manic and another who is schizophrenic. When I had the chance, I came close to the two guides and asked, "Are you going to be okay?" I nodded in the direction of their two liabilities.

"We'll be okay."

We left the smoky building, its leaky canvas and bulging tarp, and retreated up the hill. We hung our rain gear under our tarp, peeled off a damp outer layer of clothing and hung that up too. Jean had opened the waterproof pack liner and thrown the sleeping bags and Therm-a-Rest pads into the tent earlier when I had pulled out the stove and supper items.

As we were about to enter the tent, I could hear the way off thrum of radial aircraft engines. "DC-3," I thought as the sound came closer. Then I saw it, a DC-3 between me and the hill across the river, squeezed between the cloud deck and the river, just a bit higher off the water than our tent. I looked across the river to the south, where the patches of fog and smoke still rested. He was going up the river into that stuff. A pilot using the river as his only road home. "I hope he makes it," I thought, and I climbed inside the tent—our comfortable and dry sanctuary.

Easy sleep did not come right away. My thoughts were first tangled by the predicament of the DC-3 pilot. Flyers in that part of the world perform their work for a public imbued with the deluded belief that "bush pilots" are infallible. Already that summer there had been two accidents with multiple fatalities. Neither had shaken that public view. I was worried about the pilot and others on the plane. But there was nothing that I could do about it from our tent at Williams Creek.

Then I thought about the two guides, strong creative women, eager to see if fresh pizza could come out of a sandy hole in the middle of a pouring rain. Could they cope with their two disabled men while leading the rest of their crew safely to Dawson? The few words we had spoken together indicated that they would cope. So I tried to put that issue out of mind as I tossed in my sleeping bag.

Then, at last, I came to the issue that must have been troubling my sleep: That canvas! How had that canvas survived as the room ceiling? That roof had been leaking for years, wet cotton canvas would not have lasted that long, and why put up a canvas ceiling in that kind of building in the first place? After all, it had only been a machine shop or forge. Forge? Forge?? That ceiling was asbestos cloth!

After that I slept deeply.

In the morning we packed up, and joined our acquaintances for breakfast. I climbed up and cut off a corner of the "canvas" ceiling and holding one edge of it with a fork I put it over the flame on our stove. It smoked a bit as the grime of many years burned off. Gradually the fiber ends reddened in the flame but the fabric remained untouched. "Asbestos," I announced to the group around me. As apprehension concerning our surroundings rose amongst the travelers, I then explained that the asbestos ceiling was so wet that it was unlikely to pose a threat of airborne asbestos particles.

A few days later we stopped for lunch at a place where someone had cut into the river bank with a large bulldozer. The scar was several years old and there was no sign that the track had been recently used. While enjoying our meal, I spotted a fragment of fabric poking out from the groove cut by the dozer blade. I pulled on it and delivered a foot or two of cloth. It was the same type of stuff that had been on the ceiling at Williams Creek. The bulldozer had found it where it had lain buried in the riverbank for a long time.

It was a strange coincidence. More asbestos cloth. No sign of any building. No sign of any human activity other than the short dozer track back into the brush. Was the track part of a search for minerals? This was not likely. It was a mystery!

We pulled off the river at Eagle, Alaska and eventually arrived back in Whitehorse where we had left our truck. While there we decided to take the tour of the restored Klondike II, one of the last and certainly the most impressive of those paddle wheelers that plied the Yukon. The restoration was well done, and the person in charge of selecting guides for the summer season must have had a connection with an excellent school of drama. Our guide spoke his lines as if he were using his job as a precursor to a career on Broadway. We wended our way through the boat, hearing about design of the steam engines, the quality of the furnishings, and about steamboat travel in general.

Klondike II was built to replace the original Klondike that had been wrecked. Steamboats on the Yukon, and on most rivers, wrecked more often than one might imagine. Going down river in any kind of powered boat it is all too easy to run up on a bar, have the current push the boat ever higher, while swinging the stern around to put the boat sideways across the river. The impeded water mounds up on the upstream side, comes over a low point and your time on that boat is finished.

Toward the end of the tour we emerged onto the top deck behind the pilot house and below the twin stacks that led to the fireboxes for the boilers. Near the stern was a collection of buckets and fire fighting tools. Our guide explained that one of the hazards of steamboat travel was fire. I remembered the Currier and Ives prints showing famous steamboat races in which the stacks of racing river boats spouted fire into the night sky. Even when not racing, coals and sparks from the stacks could land on the upper deck and produce a conflagration before anyone noticed. I looked down at the deck under my feet. It was comprised of tongue and groove boards identical to that rough ceiling at Williams Creek. On top of the tongue and groove board, protecting it from fire, was a layer of asbestos cloth. It had been painted with gray deck paint, but there was no doubt what it was. The ceiling of the building at the Williams Creek Mining Co. had been made from the deck of a wrecked or abandoned steamer, ripped off and turned upside down.

The dozer cut in the bank? I wonder if someone, knowing that a steamboat wreck had occurred at that site, went looking for it. If they did, they missed the clue provided by that scrap of asbestos cloth.

And the guy who couldn't take it any longer? We learned that he had walked out from Little Salmon, hitched to Dawson City, signed into a bed and breakfast, and had been doing a lot of sleeping.

Inventory

FOR LONG TIME I THOUGHT that I would never be thrown by a horse. Then in one year I was thrown twice. I should have known that if I rode enough sooner or later that I would be thrown. Call it what you will—optimism, over-confidence, arrogance, or the mindset of the tin-horn dictator—I surely had a fall coming.

For some reason, I never thought this way about rapids. I knew that someday there would be a long swim. Of course, I didn't know when it would happen; only that when it did it would be entirely my fault. Those who are thrown from a horse can blame the horse. It is unreasonable to blame a river. And swims, like being thrown, can be dramatic.

When we kneel for a rapid in the security of our canoe, we watch as the water-covered boulders and ledges flash by inches below our knees. Skillful path finding through the turbulence is a joy to experience. In our euphoria we must remember that the rocks we see represent the essence of our world; beautiful but, underneath the veneer of beauty, hard and indifferent to our accomplishments. I find some people who have no understanding of this reality. They live with the attitude that they and their ideas will always float suspended in the veneer that is so kind to humans. Those who I listen to and respect are the ones who, from time to time, have suddenly found themselves outside the canoe and have survived the trip.

Snake Rapid on Quebec's Dumoine River is a Class II that has a nice path of moderate water going right, then left, and then right. By the time Jean and I ran it in 1986 we had paddled enough to know that we could do the rapid, but not enough to have solid braces or to read water well. When we hit, we leaned the wrong way, failed in our brace, and then, to make our paddling companions feel better about our competence, we swamped over the downstream side.

The canoe rolled over, we plunged under the foam with the loose fitting life jackets riding up under our chins, and we were off. Surfacing we located each other and the canoe. As we bumped along over the stream boulders, taking the repeated hits on our butts and legs, we did a few things right (getting to the upstream side of the boat and holding onto our paddles) and other things wrong (holding onto the canoe instead of the painters). The canoe, upside down and buoyed up by the gear tied inside, suddenly hung up on a ledge, and we were jerked free. A hundred feet further on, we dropped into a large pool at the end of the rapid. I looked upstream as our canoe gradually slid off the ledge. By now the painter was in my hand and the boat joined us once again. Several friends arrived to help us ashore.

Water gushed from the canoe, the packs, and the previously-undetected hairline crack in the plastic camera bag. Photography was cancelled for the rest of trip. The introductory portion of our first swim was over.

With the same rationale as the thrown rider who remounts his horse, we reembarked our bruised bodies and ran the next rapids easily, and the next after that. When we got to the portage at the falls, I found out just how heavy water soaked packs were. My bruised thigh cramped as I limped over the easy trail. Some lovely campsites beckoned. I was ready to stop. I knew a large Canadian party was ahead of us, and I didn't want to look for scarce campsites after dark. The wind had just shifted and rain clouds were gathering, but the others had decided that we were moving on.

The rapids below the falls were an easy run and, as the evening light poured between the now ominous rain clouds, it illuminated a shining pathway of safe water to the lake below. It was a golden chute leading to a heavenly tranquil sea. I wouldn't have missed that sight for a compound fracture.

We camped on the top of an esker about 25 feet above the water, our tent stakes crammed into the cracks between pine needle covered plum-sized stream pebbles left there by the subglacial river of a past ice age. It was raining before we got the tents up.

In my rain suit I sat with my sore legs dangling off the top of the narrow esker. Sitting, I drank hot soup and watched the water run off my pants. The Canadians were camped nearby and one of them came over to chat. They had holed one of their fiberglass canoes that afternoon and were trying to get it dry and warm enough so that a fiberglass patch could be applied. For them, this was going to be a late night.

He was a nuclear engineer at a Canadian power plant. We discussed the differences in the two types of reactors our countries had chosen to develop. He stood under our tarp taking his turn at occasionally pushing the tarp up to prevent the increasingly heavy rain from pooling. I thought it a wondrous world when nuclear engineers and doctors spend their time on top of eskers in the rain, pouring water from tarps that could have been hung by 10-year-olds.

The gussets in our plastic pack liner had blown out and most of the things in the pack were wet. (After this we got pack liners without gussets.) Inside our dripping tent we mopped the sleeping pads with a dry piece of clothing, spread our dry sleeping bag as a quilt and got under it. The heavy rain continued.

By morning the rain had stopped. The mist was heavy on the water. We paddled off into an area of steep hills that came close to the river. In the haze our perspective was lost and the hills appeared to overlap each other. Several of us recognized the similarity of the scene to ancient Chinese art. It was only when we looked at ourselves in modern plastic conveyances that we reentered the 20th century.

The wind changed direction again and a short time later the sun broke through the haze. The hills receded and the river widened into a braided flow around gravel bars. The gravel flew by under clear water as we threaded our way among the deeper channels to avoid those that would strand us.

We ate lunch on a bar, now in the full heat of the sun. Within minutes of our arrival, we emptied our packs and spread out wet belongings. Soon the bar was covered with steaming raingear, tents, clothing, and sleeping bags. We plunged into the river for a welcome swim and cleanup.

As I climbed out of the river refreshed, I spotted our gear, strewn over the pebbles, baking dry in the sun: bandannas; socks; a ball of twine; boots; a paperback book, its pages forever stuck together; shirts; maps. In fact, everything that Jean and I carried on the trip was spread out in the sun. I looked it over.

Everything there was an old friend, a familiar sight, but how much of it had we really needed, really used? Though we had paddled our gear for miles and had hauled it over rough portages, we did not need most of it. In fact, if we had picked out a few essentials we could have canoed to the end of the river in comfort and safety, leaving the rest as a surprising sight to greet the next party to canoe around the bend. If pulling our canoe ashore and emptying it was the end of the introduction to our first swim, the end of the experience itself was the view of our gear spread out to dry in the noonday sun.

That view has remained with me over the years and has returned each time when, as a cancer center director, I have spoken with patients or the public about how the diagnosis of cancer affects a person.

This inventory, this deciding what is essential and what is not, is something that a cancer patient does early in the illness. Whether cured or not, the patient initially looks at his or her life and its accompanying baggage, and decides what is and what is not important. Thereafter the patient's life is influenced by the taking of that inventory.

For most, life itself is the first thing a patient seizes. Otherwise the rest of the trip is cancelled. The tent, the canoe, the warm shirt can be left on the sandbar as long as there is life. And then, if there is time, there are family and friends—a gentle haven of sometimes tearful embraces, awkward words, shuffling feet. But family and friends. Given more time, a cancer patient notices that the country passing by looks different: the hills more friendly, the water more gentle and caring, the daybreak more precious.

So some of us who have been given the diagnosis set out again on our journey, our belongings packed securely and dry now; but our souls are a bit different for having taken an inventory. Our dunking was accidental, but came out well—just a bruise or two. It leaves us thinking of those whose inventory is reduced to a life clutched in desperation with all else left behind. We are thinking of those who have abandoned their treasure on a bar, leaving it to be found by the next party when it canoes around the bend.

South Pacific

WHEN I WAS AN UNDERGRADUATE at Dartmouth during the early 1950s there were three people who went around town in moccasins: Jack Tangerman, a diabetic classmate of mine who kept his insulin inside his parka so that it wouldn't freeze on his trips to the far north (and who eventually died from this disease); the young Indian who operated a Native American craft shop where the college museum now stands; and Art Moffat. When I came back to Dartmouth after graduation from medical school I saw the movie that had been made from the spools of film recovered from the Dubawnt River cache where Art died of hypothermia in 1955.

I had chosen Dartmouth, partly because I knew that it was a fine college. My decision was clinched because the person who put the College Catalogue together had chosen to insert a half page photo of a couple of Dartmouth students in a canoe running the Quarter Mile Rapids on the White River just a few miles from campus. This photo reached out across 1,500 miles to Omaha and lured me to a college I had never seen. It meant I could go to college and canoe, too. Finally, the father of my eighth grade sweetie had gone to Dartmouth and he could do a kick turn on skis.

Within days of my arrival I had realized that it was unlikely that I would be seeing Quarter Mile Rapids anytime soon. I was submerged in the pre-med curriculum, four afternoon labs per week and Saturday morning classes. Jack and I would pass each other from time to time.

He walked silently in his mocs, his sheathed knife at the ready on his belt, and the fringes on his leather shirt swinging silently. I clumped along with heavy books under my arm, the nylon of my cheap jacket whistling as the sleeves rubbed the body. It never entered my mind that I didn't have to be a doctor.

But I realized that I didn't have to envy Jack. Although Jack was eager to don the costume, the real McCoy was Art. Thirteen years older than Jack and me, with eyes that gazed from under brows that had seen a lot of sun, Art moved through town not as an actor but with a lithe grace suggesting that he had just put his paddle down and stepped from a canoe. At camp Vermilion the counselors had spoken with awe of the 600 miles of the Albany River in Ontario. Art had done it solo, when he was sixteen.

After a few weeks, I managed to get down to the Ledyard Canoe Club, located in a pleasant white cape with attached canoe shed and a front porch that looked out on the Connecticut River. One of the upperclassmen showed me the racks of wood /canvas and aluminum canoes, explained the rules, and, after I paid my dues, I was given a key. That key was the best thing that happened to me during my freshman year. Despite my impossible schedule I could find a free hour from time to time, slip a canoe from the rack and have a brief paddle.

There were also occasional "feeds," group dinners put together by paddlers, cooked on the wood stove in the clubhouse. While eating our spaghetti, we viewed the photos on the wall of guys running the broken Sharon Dam on the White River. And we heard stories of how in the 1930s the club members had gone to Canada, purchased a number of Chestnut canoes and then paddled them at night from Canada into the U.S. on Vermont's Lake Memphremagog, bypassing the U.S. Customs Office, thereby saving more than a hundred dollars per canoe. This eating and reminiscing was done under two large carved panels fastened to the smoke-stained walls: "He Clung to His Paddle" and "Coheraemus" (We stick together), the club motto.

As you may gather, our student society in that fall of 1949 was essentially monastic. The nearest women's college was miles away, only a handful of students had cars, and there was only one phone per dormitory. For a person on my budget, the US mail was the only practical means to communicate with a girl. Hanover, for many of us during those years, was the stateside equivalent of a sailor's life in the South Pacific during World War II so graphically described to us by older brothers or friends who had returned only four years earlier from that war.

This longing for companionship was given a boost by the nostalgic replay of that theater of the war by James Michener in his *Tales of the South Pacific*, which most of us had read and treasured. The musical based upon these stories opened in April of 1949 and the vinyl LP recording with the original cast had just come out. Many evenings we could hear strains of "There is Nothin' Like a Dame" from the room of sophomores across the dormitory hall.

Yet during the three big party weekends, those special times of the year when many of the class had dates, student behavior was not necessarily that of a sailor on leave. Coats, ties, and a confused version of medieval chivalry were common. Our dates reciprocated in kind. The average student believed that having sex got you into trouble. It was common to poke fun at the cohort of girls who lived with their student husbands in housing that had originally been developed for the married veterans. These young women pushed their baby carriages to gatherings where they exchanged comic books with one another. We didn't want that kind of wife. Condoms were sold from Fletcher's basement furniture store to the adventurous students who thought differently about this subject. Sometimes they proudly displayed their storehouse of Fletch's newest "French ticklers." These boasts were met with disgust by most of the rest of us. Abortion was illegal. What kind of girl would use a diaphragm before marriage? And The Pill was still an unfulfilled goal in the minds of scientists.

Those sophomores across the hall had a rather different take on the subject. One of them was particularly adventurous, as was his girlfriend whom he knew affectionately as "Happy Bottom." During the fall party weekend, we were astounded to witness the two of them clad in towels walking down the hall to the shower room during one of the few moments that the police officer who was on duty in the dormitory was distracted. When we learned that following their shower they had prepared for what came next by reviewing a deck of pornographic playing cards showing 52 versions of paired and group sex, it became clear that what we were witnessing was not the norm. For the rest of that weekend, we could hear, "There is Nothin' Like a Dame" over and over.

Along with this song, however, there was another: "Some Enchanted Evening." When I first heard this song, I was still humming and singing melodies from Rogers and Hammerstein's earlier hit, *Carousel*, and was not impressed by *South Pacific*. I was stuck on "If I Loved You" from *Carousel*. But as "Some Enchanted Evening" repeated itself again and again during that weekend (the perpetrators were content to let side one of the record play over and over for some reason) I began to identify with the passionate longing of Emile de Becque for Nellie. I recognized that I, too, had a desire (appropriate and legitimate, of course) for someone "across a crowded room."

Fortunately for our further evolution into manhood, my roommates and I witnessed the departure of the towel-wearing sophomore at midterm. He had spent Winter Carnival with Happy Bottom with the music from *South Pacific* once again wafting in our direction. When she returned to her college at the end of the party, he had contrived to prolong the music with two local women. By the time they left, he was looking rather the worse for wear, had loaned his precious auto to a friend who had totaled it, and then had received notice from the College that he had flunked out, just as his father arrived for a visit. His father congratulated him for staying in school as long as he had, bought him a new car, and sent him to Florida for a "vacation."

So I learned about the way the world worked from this vicarious perch, while keeping my sanity by paddling on the Connecticut and other nearby rivers. My best friends were those who enjoyed a healthy outdoor life and whose family background and social values differed from those I saw in the suite across the hall. As the months went by I obtained various part time jobs. These gave me the wherewithal to invite dates for the party weekends and I met some fine young women. Some of them were happy to paddle with me, and life as a student became more enjoyable.

I graduated from Dartmouth and moved on to medical school in Boston. In my fourth year of medicine and with internship looming I met Jean Geary. A recent graduate of Smith College, she had put her political science degree aside to type patient referral letters in the office of a Boston orthopedist. We were introduced by one of her Smith College friends, and I fell in love with her on our first date as we danced in the dining room of Vanderbilt Hall, the Harvard Medical School dormitory. We were engaged in eight weeks.

We married in June and rushed as a couple into the people-grinder that turned me into a physician in academia and Jean into the perfect wife for a person with this career choice. Ten years into our marriage we bought the square stern Grumman, and life jackets for our young family. If the three children and gear took up too much room in the boat, Sal, our Labrador, swam alongside the canoe. We were on the water, that was important. We were a family, and that was important. We were too busy. We had to be.

51

The children grew well and strong and went off to college. My reputation in academia prospered. We moved to a fine house and Jean got her horse. In 1985, while on sabbatical in Minneapolis, we took a white water course with the Rapid Riders, and I learned more about white water in a few weeks than I had learned in the previous 40 years of paddling. Life was getting better.

We sold our old Chevy truck and got a new Ford pickup with a cap and a canoe rack. One beautiful fall day in 1994 we put the air bags in our Mad River Explorer, lifted it onto the rack and headed for a reunion of the group with whom we had paddled the Ashuapmushuan River in Quebec that summer. Our share of the food and drink was in the back of the truck along with our tent and sleeping bags. There was a dam release on the Farmington River at New Boston, Massachusetts that weekend, the weather was warm, the fall colors were at their peak, and our friendship with the members of the group was as solid as friendship ever gets.

I had the radio on and prior to the broadcast of the Saturday afternoon opera, Vermont Public Radio had chosen to play some show-tune music. I heard the voice of Ezio Pinza, the bass stolen from the Metropolitan Opera in 1949 for *South Pacific*:

"Some enchanted evening, you may see a stranger..."

I looked across the cab to Jean who was curled in the corner between seatback and door, working her knitting needles and looking at me with a smile. We had been together for 37 years, but suddenly I recalled the lonely feelings from that freshman year. The emotions that caused Emile de Becque to launch into this song with the famous refrain swept over me. At that moment I knew that the pickup cab held the luckiest man in the world, so I joined in with Pinza for the final "Once you have found her, never let her go."

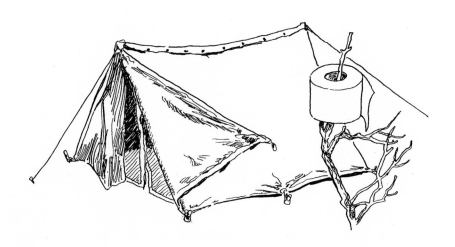

Northern Tissue

THE GREEN PUP TENT was made of waxed cotton twill and carried the musty canvas treatment smell found in war surplus stores. Its thin floor bulged upwards, lifted by the mat of balsam boughs we had layered carefully under it. Inside the front flap a few snaps attached the two panels of flimsy mosquito netting but left wide gaps—a boulevard for biting insects. It was 1957 and this was the first tent Jean and I bought. It cost $12.95.

Rain clouds rose in the west and soon lightning flashes lit up the night sky. Now, thunder caused us to wonder whether our tent-money had been well spent. At least our gear was safely stowed under the overturned canoe nearby.

A few feet away on the east the view was more comforting. The waves lapped gently on the shore of Caucomgomoc Lake which had lived up to the description in the guide book we were using: "a pleasant sheet of water." The book, written about one hundred years earlier, had not anticipated that future paddlers on the lake would arrive by car instead of by a lengthy canoe trip from a distant train station. The lake itself, however, was little changed. The guide described a pleasant campsite near a spring on this shore and now we had found it a century later.

There had been but little change in other ways as well. Although zippers had been in common use since the 1930s, they had not yet found their way onto the mosquito netting in tents. Our rain gear depended upon closely woven cotton impregnated with rubber, not plastic, and the food we carried was heavy. Lots of cans. No dehydration or freeze-dried here. Some things were modern, however. Our borrowed aluminum canoe was one.

Now as the rain began I wished that the twill of our tent had been as closely woven and as strong as the cotton used by the traveler who wrote our guide book. No matter how much waterproofing is used, poorly made canvas will leak. It took only a few minutes for our tent to surrender.

"Ross, I'm getting wet."

I felt bad. This was Jean's first night in a tent.

"I'm sorry. Nothing we can do about it."

In this situation I might have perpetuated the myth that was foisted on me during my own first night in a leaky tent. I could have said, "If you hadn't touched the tent wall it wouldn't be leaking." This transfer of responsibility for the leak from the manufacturer to the buyer is one of the really great feats in salesmanship. Touching the tent wall is almost impossible to avoid in small tents. By reciting the myth I could have left my wife wet and feeling guilty about it too. She also might have seen through my fiction and hated me for trying to hornswoggle her.

In an hour the rain had stopped and we slept poorly in wet but gradually warming sleeping bags.

In the morning we breakfasted and hung our wet gear around the fire to dry. There was no warmth from the sun, for a solid deck of gray clouds had arrived. Soon it was raining again, not a thunderstorm this time, but a continuous, no nonsense all day soaker. We loaded up and headed back up the lake. While the rain beat down that night we slept in the car.

We were greeted by the sun the next morning, spent a few hours drying our gear, and embarked once again. Before we reached the end of the lake and could make our turn into the stream coming out of Round Pond, it was pouring rain again. The logging camp at the south end of Caucomgomoc had a deserted look, but as we approached it a man stepped from one of the buildings. He walked out onto the dock and motioned for us to come over.

"Want to stay inside tonight?"

We accepted his offer. He took us to a small cabin, opened the door and we entered a room in which an oil drum stove and a couple of chairs took center stage. Around the walls were several bunk beds. A clothes line hung from the rafters and a pile of dry wood was on the porch. A piece of heaven.

Our host was the caretaker of this unused camp owned by Great Northern Paper Company. Like many of those graying single males posted to remote locations by such companies, he was happy to have someone to chat with. He pronounced Millinocket with an "aw" replacing the "o" the same way that Ross McKenney did. Ross, who had advised that we approach Allagash Lake via the portage from Round Pond, was a Maine native with enough experience in the lumber industry to have lost four fingers in a sawmill accident. With this as background he became a celebrated Maine guide, performer in outdoors shows, builder of cabins and lodges, and ultimately the woodcraft advisor to the Dartmouth Outing Club.

One evening a few weeks before our trip, I had called on Ross to ask for his advice. I accompanied him while he walked along the rows of potato plants in his vegetable garden applying a fungicide spray. The missing finger tips did not impair his ability to work the Indian Pump used for spraying and one by one he described various routes for crossing between the Penobscot and St. John watersheds. We had decided on this one, and now we were here listening to someone from "Millinawket."

As a member of a crew that worked with McKenney while building a log cabin, I had learned enough about the woods and lumber camps to keep a conversation going with this lonely caretaker. It was paying off as the crackling fire in the drum stove started to warm the cabin and dry us out. Once satisfied that we were in good shape and talked out, our new friend, the caretaker, returned to his cabin.

During a pause in the rain late in the afternoon we walked out along the shore. We hadn't gone far when the rain began again. As we returned toward the camp a canoe appeared out of the rain. The two paddlers in it were dressed in olive drab ponchos that covered them from head to foot except for the side vent from which their arms emerged to hold their paddles. They came closer to shore and we could now see the packs surrounded by water in the bottom of their canoe. Although their rain gear was far better than ours, they were in for a damp night.

"Hey, we have a cabin at the logging camp. Want to join us?"

So that night Great Northern Paper Company had two couples as guests. During libations to celebrate our good fortune, I learned that the bow paddler in the new canoe was the older sister of a high school acquaintance of mine in Nebraska. Retiring to our rough bunks at the end of a happy and dry evening, we resolved to use only Northern Toilet Tissue from that point on.

Eventually the rain stopped and we went on to Round Pond and Allagash Lake. We sharpened some spruce twigs that served as pins to hold the faulty mosquito net together and I made my last balsam bed of that or any other trip. When the last cans in the heavy food pack were emptied, we returned home feeling happy. Happy enough so that a few months later we took the same tent for another trip. On that trip we again slept in the water. Later, the tent was used to cover a hay baler. It wouldn't keep that dry either.

After that early trip Jean and I learned to be comfortable in the conditions that were so challenging for us on Caucomgomoc. We bought army surplus ponchos—nylon with an impregnable coating, and snaps that could convert the pair of them into a semblance of a pup tent, if needed. They kept us dry on several trips but then an experienced canoeist asked us if we had ever tried swimming in a poncho. After that they stayed on the shelf when we went canoeing. Instead we wore rain jackets that were large enough so that life vests (PFDs to some) could fit under them. A dry life jacket provides additional insulation on a cold day, and it is not necessary to remove the life jacket each time the rain starts on those days with a mix of sun and rain.

We have had a number of tents, all of them costing more than $12.95 and each shedding rain wonderfully if correctly managed. We followed Cliff Jacobson's recommendation that a waterproof ground cloth belongs inside the tent on top of the floor, not under it. Each season I cut up a blue tarp so as to fit the tent floor with enough left over to rise against the walls on all sides. It is amazing to sleep dry when pools of water have formed under the tent.

Polyurethane and silicone waterproof coatings eventually gave us strong light-weight fabrics for tents and rain gear. Our menu changed to nutritious foods that are light and easy to carry. The modern pack weighs a fraction of what it once did, and the food tastes better. Boats are lighter and easier to carry, too. I don't have to smoke a pipe to keep the black flies at bay. DEET and my headnet do that.

But with these changes there have been others. There are now too many people and too many roads. Had it not been for the farsighted planning and hard negotiation leading to the preservation of the Allagash waterway, canoe tripping in that area would be over.

In daytime beyond the ribbon of uncut firs along the conserved Allagash waterway, one now hears the diesels of industrial logging. But at night, one can still stay in the quiet of a campsite near the spring described in a 150-year-old guidebook. It has not been bulldozed for a road and the trees have been spared. One can imagine the old boys sitting at the fire in this campsite with tobacco and grease keeping the bugs at bay. You can smell the spruce smoke on the camper's woolen clothes and the whiskey on their breath. Behind them is their tent, 40 pounds of tightly woven cotton. Far off, one can hear the first rumble of summer thunder. A promise of rain.

But then the image fades. The Great Northern cabins are gone and so is the gray-haired caretaker. The horses that pulled the sleds of pulp wood are gone. Many of the paper mill smoke stacks are cold. Great Northern Paper Company is defunct. Northern Tissue is now made by Georgia Pacific Company, and it comes in a new "gentle" quilted form. And my obligation to buy it has passed.

Northern Tissue

Responsibility

A T THE END OF THE LEDGE a rushing tongue of water leaped into space and then, falling, tore itself apart on the rocks below. The roar of the river, coupled with the micro-climate induced by the atomized water and the splendid view of cascades above and below this spot, had invited us to stop for the view. The sun was bright, fair weather clouds sailed the blue sky, and the fine breeze held the insects at bay.

Even when a portage is mandatory, it is the second nature of a canoeist to examine a falls from the standpoint of what might be done to lessen the consequences of a plunge over it. Paddlers usually do this silently, not verbalizing the details about their planning in this regard, but looking into their faces as they peer toward such water, one can follow their eyes as they weigh the options for canoe or paddler. Opportunities existed where well-planned and executed actions might have delayed injury or death, even in this maelstrom, but as the eyes swept the length of the falls, it was obvious that calamity would be inevitable.

Jean and I let the others move on and for a bit we sat quietly. After a moment she pointed just behind me to an inch-long toad that had hopped clumsily from a crack in the rock. The toad moved along, coupling lightning fast hops with moments of still repose. At first its motion appeared chaotic, but over time it became apparent that the toad was headed toward the lip of the precipice beneath which the water surged. Closer and closer toward its doomsday the toad hopped.

Jean and I looked at each other, and without speaking shared the wordless understanding that grows from many years of a loving marriage. The issue was whether to turn the toad back from its suicidal path or, because we were intruders into his world, to let Mother Nature's design prevail. With simultaneous gentle shrugs we agreed to let Mother Nature win.

The toad continued its advance, now sliding into a small cleft in the lip over the falls. Here a spider had suspended its web from the thin branches of low blueberry bushes rooted in the crack. The toad edged farther out on the small patch of slippery duff collected in the crevice. Below, and out of focus, the cataract raged. In this impossibly precarious position, there was a sudden movement. The proof that it was the flip of the toad's tongue lay in the disappearance of a fly that had been struggling in the web. The toad's jaw closed and with a careful turn it hopped the path back to its shelter.

One reason the canoeist takes river trips to remote areas is that decisions like the one Jean and I made about the toad can occur without prejudice. If I had been watching that toad's erratic progress toward the edge of the parapet on our medical center, I would have been obliged to "save" it. We are moving in our anthropocentric culture toward a time when one's duty toward that world is not fulfilled if toads are allowed to slip over the brink. It should be recognized that even at times when it seems needed, human intervention may be harmful. In the case of the toad, we would have denied it a free dinner.

At the beginning of the portage trail above the falls, the Province of Quebec has placed a small sign naming the falls. This is the only sign on the entire river, despite the presence of other potentially fatal hazards. The sign does not declare "Danger!" or carry other warnings. If the sign had not been there, there would have been no problem finding the portage trail. I was grateful to the Province for allowing me to sit where I could watch the toad. There was no fence, or other restraint either. If

I had tumbled in, there would have been no lawsuits or recriminations. No jury could back the contention that there was inadequate documentation of danger. Had I been deaf and blind, the reverberating air and mist generated by the falls would have conveyed danger.

Such restrained signage is in contrast to Yosemite National Park, where not too long ago a macho young man cavorted at the top of Bridalveil Fall until he slipped. Desperate, he grabbed his girlfriend. They both went over together. The response to this accident included more signs and stronger fences that disgraced this otherwise awe-inspiring spot. The rationale for such steps seems to indicate a national policy that seeks to preserve the DNA code for recklessness in the American gene pool.

Several years later, thoughts of toad suicide returned to me as we unloaded our boats at West Stewartstown, New Hampshire for a five day, four night canoe trip in March. There had been rain and snow in the early morning, and the upper Connecticut River was high and fast. We had decided not to put in further up-river where the white water was more challenging. Four of the party were college students with little canoe experience. It was spring and the water was cold.

The other four members of the party were retired college faculty with plenty of river trips behind them. This trip was designed simply for young and old to enjoy a spring paddle on the Connecticut River. Although one of the group had invited the students and had organized the food, there was no formal "leader," nor had any discussion occurred as to whether teaching the younger members paddling or river skills was a goal of the trip.

The results of this informal approach could have been predicted. First, there was a long wait at a crossroads where the two vehicles carrying the party planned to meet. There was no phone service at this spot, so the late party could not call the waiting party about a delay. Then, as the canoes came off the college student's car, we noted that they lacked bow and stern lines. We cut some rope to correct this problem, but the rope was not the kind that would float. To waterproof their packs the students had drawn garbage bags over the outside of their packs, not inside where they would be protected from damage.

In good spirits we set off, not with an experienced paddler in each boat to educate a novice partner, but with the experienced and novices in separate canoes. The first upset occurred at the first landing of the day and those dunked had clothing that was cold when wet. That night, warmed by the fire at a campsite on a small island, I did a bit of teaching. I began with a discussion of the whys and wherefores of bow and stern lines that would float. I then told them that cotton clothing is a bad source of warmth on a cold wet day. When we finished, one of the students scrambled up a twisted boxelder tree for amusement. I did not tell him that one of the grand old women of canoe tripping has forbidden anyone on her trips to climb trees. An accidental fall during tree climbing had spoiled a backcountry trip she led. An injury to one member of the party in wilderness can ruin a trip for everyone else.

In the morning we mentioned an upcoming encounter we would have with the breached Lyman Falls Dam and offered advice on running it. It didn't turn out as planned. One of the student canoes flipped in the quickwater well above the dam. The paddlers scrambled ashore while the overturned canoe and a floating yard sale of gear tumbled down river. The old timers had made no allowance for an upset in this location and tried to bring things under control. By now, students, seniors, gear and canoes were strung out along half a mile of riverbank. The two students who had not upset had pulled into shore immediately after their friends had flipped. They found a sympathetic woman in a nearby house. She drove them down river in hopes of recovering the errant canoe. They didn't , however, tell anyone about this arrangement. Meanwhile two seniors helped the students who had flipped come ashore while the others waited for the second student canoe to appear. When it did not, they worked their way upstream until they located the empty canoe. Where were those students? Well… you can get the picture.

Most of the time the Lyman Falls Dam rapid is easy and fun. At the water level we found running that day, however, a small frowning hole surged near the usual canoe path. It was a "keeper" that could have caused real trouble. Had there been a drowning, the seniors on that trip might have been posturing, "Well, I thought that you were going to take charge."

At the very beginning when the boats without painters came off the car, someone should have said, "I can see we have a serious problem with this trip. Now what we all have to do is to make certain that no one spoils it for the rest. I don't especially want to act as a trip leader, so let's agree as a group that there are some things we have to do right now to make this trip as safe as we can. OK?…" Silence. "OK. Step one…"

On the other hand, some students don't learn until they have made the mistake; and one theory of education says that a "teaching moment" accompanies a mistake. No mistakes allowed, no teaching. It worked for old Engle when he taught me to turn a canoe.

But Engle had acted responsibly as he taught me. If I had missed coming ashore on that point and had been blown out into the lake, he would have fired up the Johnson and been after me. So when this type of teaching is used, it is important that the teacher have a plan to recover when things go wrong. None of the seniors approaching the Lyman Dam knew that there was a hole there that day. We should have.

A couple of nights later when two of the students announced that they had to get back to Hanover by eight the next morning, we could have said, "That's a poor idea. Either you stay or you have to convince all of us to go." Instead they moved off into the dark after a late supper with about 30 miles to paddle before dawn. We let them go. Even if they paddled past Hanover in their sleep, it was unlikely that they would go over the large hydroelectric dam at Wilder. It was raining, though, and the temperature was in the 40s—a bad combination for neophytes.

That grand old woman of canoe tripping, Barbara Cushwa, would have started with the bow and stern lines. Until they were right, those students would not have been allowed in their canoe. She would have told the students that the lines had to float, described the optimal diameter, and specified the proper length for them—enough to do their work but not long enough to entrap the paddler. Then she would have insisted that the students never let their line knot. After an upset the knot would jam in an underwater rock crack at the worst possible moment. After that she would have gone on to the next of her rules. Step by step she would make them canoeists.

Some students would listen to this monologue and would understand and appreciate the reasons for rules. Others would climb a tree. And part of growing up, of becoming an expert, is to know what it is like to paddle into the dark on a cold night with leaky raingear.

Portrait of the Canoeist
as a Nude Woman

IN THE 1930S WHEN MY PARENTS SPENT A SUMMER in Boston they were invited to a picnic with a group of Appalachian Mountain Club members. Held on the shores of a quiet pond in Massachusetts and attended by a number of faculty from Harvard Medical School, it promised relief from city heat. Upon arrival at the spot, however, my parents, visitors from Nebraska, were quite surprised when their hosts stripped to the buff and plunged in. Even more surprisingly, the group ate lunch in the raw.

During that same summer, I had decided at age three that it would be cooler without my sun suit while I followed my parents in their walk across the Boston Common. After witnessing the chuckles of oncoming pedestrians, my parents turned to find me dragging the suit by its straps behind me. Despite its reputation for book banning and other blue-nose restrictions, my parents thereafter regarded Boston, and especially the Appalachian Mountain Club, as a bulwark guarding one's right to free expression.

Many years after those events, Jean and I joined with others on a small wilderness island and watched the Beaver as it taxied down the lake. It turned, the engine revved, the floats rose on the step, came free, and it was gone. I turned and found our trip leader without her clothes. I thought, "Welcome to an AMC canoe trip."

71

It was a lovely day. We loaded the canoes and headed a few miles south to the lake's outlet. Along the way our leader sitting tall in her solo canoe maintained her composure while I gradually lost mine. I assumed that she would get an awful sunburn, but after a few surreptitious glances decided that there was little risk of that. She was tanned. She was also good looking, had a bubbling personality, and clearly possessed leadership ability. We arrived at the lake outlet where, amongst some grand pines, the nine of us set up camp on the soft ground.

"Hey, look what I found!" Our leader held up a black Speedo swim suit that a previous camper had left hanging on a limb. It was clearly intended for an adolescent male. With some effort she struggled into it and, now in her equivalent of formal attire, began assisting with dinner.

On lots of canoe trips Jean and I have taken noon lunch time dips, discretely entering the water off to one side of the group, backs turned to the rest of the party, exiting with towels at hand, etc. as have most of our canoeing friends. This woman was different. There was no flouncing of the exhibitionist, no pouting of the porn star. We were witnessing pure uncomplicated nudity. On the second day of the trip, we encountered a party of Boy Scouts and their leaders. For the first time, our leader put on her life jacket in flat water. We went around the bend, and off it came. It was a hot day. Many days it was too hot for the Speedo.

Sticking to her principles, through good weather and bad, she led us. Bit by bit, as we moved along the river, group inhibitions were being rubbed off on sand beaches, deep water bends with gravel bottoms, and in swirling potholes. Although Jean and I continued to turn our backs, we were much less circumspect than previously. "After all," we said, "what the hell?" I was delighted to see the steady crumbling of restraint affecting a most attractive woman, far younger and certainly more innocent than our leader.

Our route was on a river with a long history of log drives. As a result some portages were wide enough so that large boats could be winched over them. After a night of camping along a portage, we sat around the fire for a leisurely breakfast. I had a hundred yard view down the wide trail to the river below the rapid. The path was overarched by the lush green of hardwood leaves, and the sun bounced brilliantly off the water at the bottom of this tunnel. Silently, two figures stepped into view near the water. Backlit by the reflected light, but in no need of a fill flash had I been lucky enough to have been holding a camera, the two women walked slowly side by side up the path and into our breakfast. It was beauty, pure and simple, and alive.

Guide and Client

TOM COCKED HIS BODY TO THE RIGHT in the driver's seat, lifted his left foot and its sandal to the dashboard near the light switch and stretched his back. It was an automatic and he didn't need his foot for the clutch. The desert road rose to the west. The loaded van wallowed over the blacktop undulations, as Tom flopped the loose steering wheel from side to side. The canoe trailer bucked behind the van. A quarter mile in front of us a similar van, four canoes on its top, did the same. As we approached the top of the grade, it disappeared in a cloud of white smoke.

The desert heat and the heavy load were too much for its cooling system. The transmission fluid had boiled and overflowed onto the exhaust manifold. That is how skywriting airplanes make smoke, putting oil into the manifold. Neither we nor the van ahead slowed down. The top of the grade was near, and this was Texas.

There are many reasons why it makes sense to sign up with an outfitter for some trips. I was seeing one of them now. It was not my van, and I hadn't had to drive it all the way from New Hampshire to West Texas. Nor would I have thought to reinforce the roof of my vehicle by welding in ugly angle-iron trusses to support the four canoes and three hundred pounds of baggage up there. It was 1993 and we were on our way to the Rio Grande.

As we had put the boats on the rack, I noted that they were like outfitter canoes generally—some new, some old, some in between and one

75

so decrepit it was sure to be its last trip. We slowed, then stopped at a crossroads where a Latino had parked his pickup. We got out and stretched while Tom unloaded an Old Town Discovery that apart from a dimple or two looked new. The Mexican gave Tom some bills and we were underway again. Tom's last trip through the lower canyon of the Rio Grande had been immediately after spring break weekend. He had recovered two pinned canoes abandoned by student revelers, sold one immediately and now he had sold the second.

The road dead-ended at a closed vanadium mine across the Rio Grande and the border at La Linda. The Mexican customs agents on duty scarcely looked up from their card game before resuming it. We piled gear and boats on the riverbank, and the vans drove off. (My trip notes record, "It is not a good idea to leave vehicles in La Linda overnight.")

A lot may be learned about a group from the way that it loads boats and embarks. Our performance indicated that we ranged from novice to competent and from out of shape to athletic. On trips we have organized with friends, safety depends to a great extent on the judgment and skills of all the participants. Here our safety was going to depend upon Tom and his wife who were our guides, and the leadership they provided. This fact was made clear when Tom instructed us to tie our gear in the canoes in a fashion that would let him cut individual packs free one at a time if the canoe got pinned. On trips with our friends, a rescue would fall to the group, and the way we tie things is different.

Within a mile or two, the two women paddling a Dagger Legend were being blown about by the upstream wind. Jean and I were reassigned to that canoe so that the women could have a boat with less rocker. This helped some, but with a straighter hull their boat now had a desire to go straight in the turns, and there were many turns. Rimming the undercut banks and hanging over them in the turns was a heavy growth of cane. Going wide in the turns meant some abraded skin and, because of the desire of paddlers to lean away from the cane, a risk of upset. I felt sorry for these two as the afternoon went on.

For a time I believed that a person who could not do a J-stroke (or the pry equivalent), should not go on a river trip. Then I encountered a couple of experienced long distance trippers who never used the J-stroke or pry. Instead they turned the other face of the stern paddle to the water for control, what the counselors at Camp Vermilion called "ruddering." Some who paddle long distances, claim it is a more efficient stroke. Others refer to it as the "goon stroke," however. Most long-distance paddlers use a smooth pry believing that it allows a higher cadence and therefore increased power delivery. There is no greater inducement to learning these strokes than to be put on a winding river in an upstream wind.

That evening, we finally got to know our companions on the trip. Their experience on rivers varied from great to nonexistent. They came from diverse backgrounds and interests. Linked by fascination with nature and desert ecology, they had self-selected for this trip, and were expecting a good time. One of the two women who had been blown about for the afternoon turned out to be in school administration. A bit on the heavy side, with a physique more suited to budget management than outdoor adventure, I was surprised that she had signed up for this trip. We talked over high school education, teacher motivation, and other topics while the mesquite fire burned down. The meal had been excellent, and with no bugs in the air and no risk of bad weather, the group bedded down on the sand. The West Texas night sky is dark. I had no idea that satellites crossed the night sky so frequently.

When we came a few days later to the most technically difficult rapid in the canyon, Tom had a ready-made solution to it. He and his wife stood a few feet apart on the ledge at the top and a good paddler brought the loaded canoe down to the ledge between them. The two caught the boat as it arrived on the ledge and held it while the paddler scrambled out. Two of us stood in the water below the ledge and received the bow of the boat over the ledge. Once the canoe was down we threw the bow and stern lines to the school administrator who stood on a large boulder across the pool. When she had the lines in hand we let go of the canoe.

I had some concerns about this arrangement. I felt that a person with lots of experience should have been assigned to stand on the boulder and do the lining. The force of the current pushed against the upstream face of the boulder and I was sure that the loaded canoe would scrape across the face of the boulder—a reasonable chance for a hang-up.

We released the first canoe and it was picked up by the current. When it had a bit of momentum, our administrator gave the stern line a solid yank, pulling the stern closer to the boulder and tipping the bow out into the stream. Now placing some tension on the bow line, the canoe ferried out away from the boulder and slipped downstream. Perfect! She handed the bow line to the person downstream who took the boat from her and awaited the toss of the line from the next canoe. Too much set on the boat and she would have lost it. Not enough and it was on the boulder. I was amazed.

I never found out where she had acquired her skill. Did she play with wooden boats in a backyard stream as a kid? Pushing them into currents with a long stick? Had she floated fishing lures into downstream eddies? Or had getting budgets past the voters trained her to take advantage of momentum and currents? I hope that this was not her last trip. She will make an excellent paddler, once she can do the J stroke.

A View of Bridges From the Water

THOSE WHO ARE SERIOUS PADDLERS become familiar with the bottom of bridges, a sight that people on the road or railroad tracks above miss. This view into the undergarments of a bridge provides the paddler with information about the economic health and priorities of the community the bridge serves. A well-maintained bridge is usually easy to spot. Bridges with rusty components ready to fall may be sufficiently threatening to make us paddle faster. In addition, the view from a canoe or kayak can often tell us why a spot was picked for the bridge, why a particular bridge design was chosen for that location, and may cause us to learn more about the history of river crossings in this place.

In my years of paddling, I have found friendly bridges, soaring bridges, and utilitarian bridges. I have found bridges so low that I couldn't paddle under them. Once, I got out of the canoe and let it float empty beneath the bridge before re-boarding on the downstream side. I have seen the low farm bridge on Otter Creek in Vermont that captured and killed a professor. On another river, I passed the sharp face of a pier that folded a boat around the legs of person who was the subject of a dramatic rescue. I have seen abandoned stone bridges resembling the ancient ruins depicted in the background of famous Renaissance paintings, and bridges under construction with the bustle of concrete pouring and sharp reinforcing bars. That I remember so many of them suggests that each has been important to me.

So I will tell you about my lessons from three of these many bridges: one on an interstate highway, a utilitarian bridge; one in the far north, a bridge that suits its valley well; and one in a faraway land, a bridge that was never finished.

The Weber is a short Utah river that originates west of the Uinta Mountains and east of the Wasatch Range. It runs north through two reservoirs before dropping to the west through Weber Canyon. Here it is accompanied by the Union Pacific Railroad tracks and Interstate 84. After passing through Ogden it enters the Great Salt Lake in a delta where impoundments provide habitat to abundant migratory waterfowl.

If one can accept the lacerated Royalex which is inherent in canoeing amongst the razor-sharp rocks on the Weber, it provides an exciting afternoon of whitewater fun. Jean and I paddled it in 1997 in a tandem canoe. Our son was in his inflatable kayak and our ride culminated in a run under Interstate 84 in Weber Canyon. As the highway snakes down through the narrows, one curve is built on a bridge that carries the highway out over the entire width of the river and then returns the road to the same side of the river from which it just left. The bridge is supported on columns that seem to go on forever.

For us the huge concrete posts offered a giant slalom in water that was boiling along. Overhead, the sun disappeared and was replaced by a low roof of concrete and steel. The roar of water was now combined with the thrum of diesels and whistle of high-pressure tires on pavement: Peterbilts, Freightliners and Macks rushing goods to market only a few feet above our heads. The only thing that might have provided more excitement for us would have been a runaway 100-car freight train in the canyon while we canoed.

The pure exhilaration that such an experience produces often gives way later to a different, more contemplative mood. It should if we are to stay out of trouble, for prolonged exhilaration corrupts judgment. We need exhilaration, but in measured doses.

82

This bridge forced me to contemplate rivers and bridges: pure untrammeled free-flowing rivers devoid of human manipulation; and bridges, the products of inspired engineering that represent a pinnacle of human achievement. I continue in a struggle to harmonize the two concepts.

The designers of the Interstate 84 bridge in the canyon were highway engineers whose job it was to fit the bridge into the narrows while leaving enough room for the Union Pacific tracks and the river water—and to do this job at the least cost. The view of the bridge through a car windshield is that of a turn in a highway and guard rails. The river briefly disappears under the bridge and then returns, a prisoner held momentarily and then released from the grip of the civil engineers. You have to be on the water to experience the redeeming qualities owned by that bridge.

When I paddle, feeling at one with the river, I question whether the bridges I see are presumptuous intruders, an assault on the river's freedom, its birthright. I fall into the habit of many others who have personified rivers—who have glued human attributes to them. I know they can teem with animal and plant life within their "bosom," but their essence is really nothing more than a lot of slippery water molecules carrying things on their way downhill. The river is not truly a living organism.

But it is hard to disagree with those who hold that the thread-like brook that dances down from an alpine hillside resembles a child, and that the winding river midsection of sturdy current with accompanying boils and eddies resembles mid-life. And who would argue that the silt-choked curmudgeonly flowing river of the delta doesn't resemble old age.

So I struggle with my question. Do the works of man violate some inherent right of the river to be a river? And I get the answer, "Only if man, in charity, gives the river those rights."

"What might those rights be?"

"To be treated with respect."

Far north of Weber Canyon, I look at a different bridge. The girders soar high above me. The span rests comfortably between the bluffs that pinch the river in this spot. It is graceful and fits the river and its valley perfectly. Despite its remote location someone took the effort and the time to design a bridge that allows me to be comfortable with it and its river.

This was wild country when the crossing was chosen. Before the highway was bulldozed through the forest, someone had to choose which of the primitive tracks left by the very few that traveled this territory was the right one for the highway to follow. An experienced bridge engineer had to study the sites for this bridge. The soil under the bridge abutments had to be free of permafrost and the river bottom solid enough to support the piers that carried the load. Only when all that was done, and the steel, concrete, and other materials had been hauled to the site from hundreds of miles away could skilled workers erect the bridge.

Now Jean and I stood next to our canoe on the sandy beach below the bridge. We were surrounded by our river gear, the next part of our journey made possible by the highway and bridge above us. Our truck and hired driver had departed for a town down the river and we were experiencing the wonderful anticipation that comes with trip departure.

But the birds. The damn birds. From nests on the girders high above, the swallows, their space invaded by canoeists, now swooped low, their throats making angry threats. As more and more were called to action in each moment, their cries increased as did their brave strafing runs. I saw spatters of white appearing on our gear as we hurried it into the canoe. Now the canoe was being hit.

"Damn birds, let's get out of here fast!"

Then I noticed that the top had come off the bottle of sun-screen that I had in my shirt pocket. The splotches of white were mostly, maybe all, sunscreen that I had been spilling. The birds were okay. The problem was me; the bridge was not part of a conspiracy supporting dive bombers. We paddled away, the birds settled down, and the bridge was left behind as the river made its first turn.

I found the unfinished bridge in 1961 when, with Jean and two children in tow, I was sent by the U.S. Public Health Service to Dhaka, East Pakistan (now Bangladesh). Assigned as a physician in the Pakistan-SEATO (Southeast Asia Treaty Organization) Cholera Research Laboratory, I spent a year of my enlistment devoted to the prevention and treatment of cholera. That is how I got to know the Ganges delta, a place where year after year cholera persists, the result of delta geography, millions of people, and rudimentary sanitation.

The Ganges and Brahmaputra waters are collected from a vast region along the southern flank of the Himalayas. The two join to form the huge delta of the Ganges. This drainage includes the wettest areas on the earth, the Cherrapunji Scarp in the Khasi Hills where the average rainfall is 40 feet per year. One year the rainfall in Cherrapunji was 75 feet. Floods are common.

The people of the delta are Bengali, unified by their language, their culture, and by the frequent natural catastrophes they face. They are divided by their religion, Islam in the east and Hindu in the western parts of the delta.

The waters of the Ganges divide into numerous channels in the delta, each one constituting a major named river. Although recently a few highways have been constructed, much of the commerce in this land remains river based. The boats that ply this maze of waterways are the result of the wonderfully divergent designs perfected over a couple of thousand years in each locality. In a good evening on the water you can smell the curry spices in the drifting smoke from the cooking fires on shore. While savoring this magic experience, one must not ignore the use of this same water upstream by millions of people who bathe in it, celebrate it , drink it, consign their dead to it, or befoul it.

Dhaka is the capital of Bangladesh, the country of the eastern delta. Its airport, at 24 feet above sea level and located 75 air miles from the sea, is the highest spot in this city of eight million. On either side of the Buhriganga, the Ganges channel that flows through Dhaka, it is about 75 miles to the contour line defining 50 feet above sea level. When hurricanes move up the narrow Bay of Bengal, the waters pile up in storm surges that drown much of the country. At such times, thousands lose their lives.

If you leave Dhaka and travel along one of the narrow roads raised above the surrounding delta land, you soon arrive at a major river channel. There the road ends. This is not a land of bridges. The alluvial delta soil is without stone. To make gravel for concrete, clay is baked to make bricks which are then pounded into fragments that substitute for gravel. Cement and steel are imported. Even if the building materials were at hand, bridges in Bangladesh would be rare. Two of the major bridges in the country were constructed during British rule, and others since have been engineered by foreign firms and funded by foreign aid programs.

Constructing a reliable and lasting bridge over a major river is a demanding task. The skilled craftspeople and appropriate materials involved are only part of the essentials. Because rivers often form political boundaries, the culture must have developed to the point where, in a stable political climate, different jurisdictions can agree on where, when, and how the bridge will be built and paid for. Many of the techniques humans have evolved for resolving conflict derive from a centuries-long history of coping with the problem of whether to make crossing a river easy or to leave it hard.

So we will take the road that ends northwest of Dhaka at a river bank where a few lonely trees offer shade to the bare ground surrounding the landing (the *ghat*). This place was one of my favorite spots to visit and I went there often. To cross the river here one takes a ferry. These ferries are country boats (*nokas*), craft shaped like half an almond made of planks held one side to another by iron staples. The length of the boats is limited to a size that is easily managed by the boatman who stands on the raised stern and sculls with a single long oar.

Professor Ahmed, our Bengali teacher, described the role of the ferry in Bengali literature, particularly poetry. For generations Bengalis have come from the countryside to the city in order to find jobs. Living in the city and remitting funds to their families and loved ones in the country, they long for the few days a year when they may return to their home and hearth in the country (their *bari*). While making these journeys most will cross a number of major channels of the Ganges. When they arrive at the ghat, the ferry is seldom waiting for them. Instead, the boatman is having tea on the far bank, or is in midstream with a load of passengers. With the patience necessary to function in this society, the traveler seeks whatever shade is available, assumes the squatting position used for resting in a culture that lacks chairs, and contemplates his loneliness while waiting. Instead of reading, as one in our culture might do in this situation, the Bengali may sink into a dream-fantasy of forbidden things, or recall the verses of a poet—a poet whose inspiration came while waiting for *his* boatman.

After boarding the ferry I have a look at the other passengers. Some of these are civil servants and teachers in loose fitting white shirts and pants (*pajamas*) others are laborers and farmers in *lungis*, a sarong-like wrap around the waist. Some have bicycles (an excellent way to travel in this flat land), and others carry baskets of fruit or vegetables. Most passengers have black umbrellas to provide shade from the intense sun. In this boat a person with cutaneous leprosy is found riding to and fro. The boatman has made his charitable contribution by offering this gratis begging platform to the leper.

Out in the center of the river was a recently constructed masonry pier for a bridge that was planned to carry the road northwest from this ghat. Italy was building the bridge as a foreign-aid project and an Italian contractor had supervised the construction. Like the famous tower in the land of the donors, the pier was leaning at an alarming angle. There was no other evidence of bridge building, no abutments, no grading for an approach road, just this isolated and tipped pier.

On later visits to this *ghat*, I sat in the reverberating heat and pondered the fate of this bridge and its road. The soil of the delta is of two types: sandy silt, or silty clay. Bedrock is hundreds of feet down. The piers of other Ganges bridges don't go that far down, but rest on firmer sand at substantial depths. Somehow they must take the load and, importantly, must withstand the scouring that could uncover the base of the pier during the rainy season when the river depth and current are high. I never learned why the pier tilted. This project, like so many in a country that routinely finds itself with unsolvable problems, was simply abandoned.

The view of that forsaken and tilted tower remains in my memory. Also remaining are the memories of the people of that country—those I met in the course of my job, patients with cholera and their families. My duties took me into their homes, usually simple houses with bamboo frames and plaited bamboo walls (*kutcha*). A wooden platform served as a communal bed. Outside was a clay stove dug into the foot-pounded earth of the compound. In the shade of banana and mango trees, peace prevailed in the *bari*. With rice paddies a few steps away, fish in the river, and a few chickens and goats, these families were fed by the bounty of the land and their river.

The simplicity of this life is enviable. And simplicity is a good strategy for survival in this life on the delta. Living there carries with it the risks of fatal diseases and exposure to the full consequences of nature's occasional fury. The seasonal flood waters that nourish the delta soil are expected. Floods resulting from storm surges are rare, unexpected, and devastating to the people and their land. There are good reasons that only those who have accumulated some wealth build brick (*pucca*) houses in the delta. The *kutcha* houses are disposable and quickly rebuilt if one is lucky enough to survive the flood.

Nor does the simple life eliminate other catastrophic events. A retreat to one's *bari* will not protect a person from civil or religious strife, wars, crop failure and starvation, or corrupt governments. When a major river of the delta eats away at the ground in front of a *bari*, there is no recourse. It is abandoned. It is not in the culture of these people to develop long-term plans or complex structures. A ferry is an easier solution to a river crossing than a bridge.

I am comforted because the Italians abandoned the bridge project. Because of man's failure I know that this river will never be bridged between my *ghat* and the sea 75 miles away. Western culture and its ambitions have slugged it out with an old, old river, and the river won. The people of the delta whose only wealth lies in the land and the river's water have a history of accepting this fact.

At this point, my mind returns to the bridge in Weber Canyon. It is part of the Eisenhower Interstate Highway System, named after the president who did so much to bring it about. I see the concrete columns supporting the bridge firmly anchored in the rapid. They are crude, low-budget, strong, and ugly but doing the job for which they were designed. We, as a country, wanted the highway system. Our democracy delivered it. Thinking about it, the bridge on the Weber is a lot more than half a world away from my bridge site on the Ganges.

But perhaps we could have shown even the lowly Weber a bit more respect.

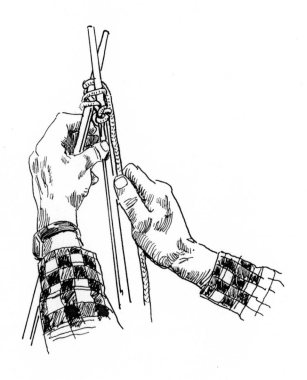

My Friend the Tarp

IT HAD BEEN A PERFECT MAINE DAY in 1989. Eddie, the shuttle driver, had told his long "shaggy coyote story" for the benefit of his passengers as we bounced along the gravel road, so the trip went fast. Now we looked out over a fine pond and the juvenile St. John River while watching the evening come on. The fire burned brightly and the pots, ready to put on the grate, were filled with good things to eat. In the west the cumulus clouds built nicely in the last of the afternoon heat. Maybe too nicely. Yes, very much too nicely.

"Think we can finish dinner before the rain hits?"

I was one of the two cooks that night and the cooks had a dual assignment: cooking and tarp rigging duty. The kitchen had been set up in an area where it would be impossible to rig a tarp in a hurry.

"Sure, if we're fast."

The pots went over the fire. Now we could see the downpour moving toward us on the hill across the pond.

"Cook! Cook!" We threatened the pasta. "Cook! You S.O.B." We could see the rain churning water on the other side of the pond. It came at us as if it were on tracks leading directly through our campfire.

"Too late!"

"Everyone, get your rain gear and forks, we are going to eat in the rain."

Jean handed me my rain gear. "Tent's shut up. Everything's inside."

93

"Thanks." I pulled it on, and noted that my hood discharged an ounce of water into our dinner every time I leaned over. Our first-night gourmet dinner was eventually served, the solid portions suspended in an unplanned soup.

The party stood about the hissing fire, rain water running off their hoods, running up their arms when they raised spoon to mouth, and trying to make me feel better. "It's OK. None of us thought it would come that fast."

They were kind.

If you can't stand being wet, you shouldn't canoe. However, there are times like meals and making/breaking camp when it is great to be out of the rain. Good tarps can make a big difference in morale. On the heavily traveled Allagash Waterway, campsite picnic tables have a fixed horizontal bar mounted over them to hold up the center of a tarp, an arrangement that acknowledges the heavy use of this route and the frequency with which loose tarp poles are destroyed by those who believe they can make a good fire with them.

Our four year old granddaughter, along for the trip with her parents, was intrigued with the success of the picnic table tarp arrangement. From Utah where it seldom rains, she found it exciting to spend several hours sitting on the picnic table watching the water pour off our tarp.

On other well-traveled rivers picnic tables and tarp poles are lacking. This is to preserve a wilderness experience on these routes so the arrangement seen on the Allagash has not been adopted. In many campsites on these rivers it is not practical or permissible to cut poles to suspend a tarp, and as most tarp stringers know, trees are not always in the right place to make a good job of it.

Carrying long wooden tarp poles from campsite to campsite is not usually feasible. What is needed are jointed poles that can be taken apart to make packing the canoe convenient. They need to be lightweight, strong and inexpensive. The steel poles sold for this purpose are heavy. The aluminum tubing sold in building supply stores is expensive and not strong enough. The answer? Aluminum ski poles that have been abused to the point where they are no longer worthy of the slopes are strong, light, and cheap.

If you don't have your own worn-out ski poles in your attic, find a skier who does, attend a yard sale at a skier's house, or talk to a ski rental store at the end of the season. They should be given to you. Don't ever pay for one!

Now remove the hand grips. First see if they are screwed on. Most screws, if present, simply hold the wrist strap on. Save the wrist strap, you may need a piece of good leather sometime. Then put the shaft of the pole between the jaws of a vise that has been adjusted to allow the pole to move easily but will not allow the grip to pass through the opening. Yank on the shaft so as to give the grip a sharp rap on the vise. The grip will come loose with one or two blows. Then remove the basket from the poles using the same approach. This may require harder raps. Save the baskets.

Once you have a pole without the basket, slip it into the end of another pole where the grip used to be. Slide the two together until they jam tightly. (Don't worry, they will come apart easily when you need to pack them.) This will give a reasonably stiff two-section pole of 6 to 7 feet in height. Of course the height depends upon the original length of the poles. You can get 7 to 9 feet by adding a third pole, but the resulting three section affair will flop about a bit. If you want a longer pole in just two sections get used poles from someone who is a cross country racer.

Most cheap tarps have grommets in their sides and corners. Good tarps have tapes instead. Put a basket over the small end of the ski pole combination and put the pointed end up through the underside of the grommet or tape opening. Fasten a line to the point of the ski pole on top of the tarp and tie it off to something solid. The line holds the tarp against the ski pole basket tying the two together.

Most tarp riggers I know attach the lines to the corner of the tarp and pull the corner out on a diagonal. This tightens the hem, the strongest part of the tarp but when it rains, water runs down the tarp sagging the single layer fabric a bit as it gets caught by the stiff hem and held back. Soon more and more water pools up stretching the fabric until it balloons downward. If not dumped the weight can sometimes bring down the tarp.

As I was pulling out the corners of my tarp one day on the Missinaibi, a friend explained how to avoid this problem. "Pull the corners out straight. Don't bother trying to tighten the hem." He was right, of course. With the corners pulled out straight, the water running down the tarp never encounters a raised edge and fails to accumulate. If the tarp is rigged this way, it may also be necessary to run several additional lines directly to the ground in addition to the lines that pull the tarp out horizontally. These prevent the edge of the tarp from flipping up in the wind. This arrangement works like a dream.

The only problem with this method of tarp hanging is that you can hardly ever rig one when you are traveling with others. If you are with a party, someone will see that the edge of the tarp is limp and move your corner lines out on a diagonal. If you rant at them while they are doing it, you may educate them. If you don't catch them in the act, however, your tarp will take on the usual mammary appearance from below as soon as it rains.

The number of poles you will use depends upon the size of your tarp and how you rig it. Generally we travel with six individual poles, enough to make three 6 to7 foot poles when assembled. We throw them into the bottom of the canoe before loading our packs. They hold the pack a bit above the bottom, and on a flatwater day, keep the pack drier.

The three poles plus a paddle or two and the available trees should get your tarp up.

Everything you take on a trip should do double duty. You will find lots of other things to do with the old ski poles. For instance, one of the best baths I ever had was inside a piece of mosquito netting held up by our ski poles while the black flies of Nunavut hummed outside. The shafts make an excellent splint for a broken tent pole (or leg for that matter), and can be used as a lever to straighten bent tent pegs.

At the Wonder Lake campground in Denali Park, an area with noteworthy rains, we noticed that some campers had reinforced their tent fly by throwing an extra tarp over it. I wondered why, until I climbed out in a middle of the night deluge and threw our cooking tarp over our tent. The lesson: Urethane waterproofing does not last forever, and you cannot predict when your tent is going to leak.

We finally had a custom tarp made that is just the right size to be rigged over our tent and a small area in front of the vestibule, our "front porch." With the tarp hung from our throw line or other rope, and propped, if necessary, by our ski poles, now we had a safe and dry kitchen. And now that we have perfected a system that suits us, it seems like it doesn't rain as much.

Other double duty items? One of my favorite examples is one described by our good friend, Ralph Baierlein. He encountered a medical student who arrived for a day of canoeing with minimal equipment: his paddle, life jacket, and a can of tuna fish. When it came time for lunch, the student ate the tuna fish with his comb.

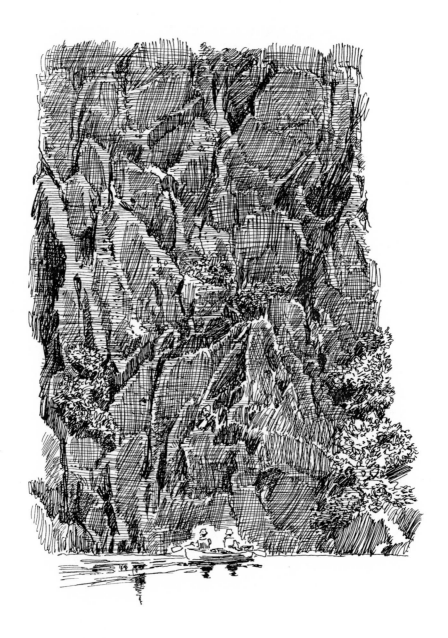

Perpetuity

A BOUT 30 YEARS AGO, JEAN AND I GRANTED a conservation easement
to the Connecticut River Watershed Council on our River Meadow
and its quarter mile of frontage on the Connecticut River. The easement
guarantees that this piece of land will never be developed, mined, oil-
rigged, or otherwise despoiled. Up and down the river a number of other
land owners have done the same.

Some have given easements to the Upper Valley Land Trust for
primitive campsites to be developed on their land. These and the river
frontage easements guarantee that canoeists have a place to stop for the
night, and also that there is some undeveloped river bank to provide the
near view. Without this near view, the distant one of forested hills dec-
orated with small villages would be lost. Nowhere else can one canoe-
camp while observing so many well-maintained buildings of the
Georgian and Federal architectural periods. From the canoe seat as you
pass these delightful towns you can see white church steeples borrowed
from the designs of Christopher Wren, each a finial to the jewel-like
town it adorns.

As I see the surveyor's tape and rebar-marked corners of newly laid
out lots along river properties, it encourages me to support organizations
that are each year preserving more of the river frontage. The conservation easements are non-revocable and are given in perpetuity. Perpetuity
is clearly a long time, but as I canoe this valley, I sometimes chuckle at
the arrogance of those who write such terms into legal documents. Only
15,000 years ago our house and most of the valley lay under the waters

of Lake Hitchcock. That 200 mile long lake, impounded by a dam generated by the earthmoving capability of the Laurentide ice sheet, stretched from Middletown, Connecticut north to St. Johnsbury, Vermont. To a geologist, reminders of this lake along with clues as to its water level at various periods are abundant throughout the valley.

For instance, the deltas of numerous streams that entered the ancient lake can now be identified in road cuts and gravel quarries throughout the region. When streams entering a lake slow, sorting of stream-carried sediments occurs. The denser materials are left on the early and steeper part of the delta while the fine material is carried out to the more gradual delta slope or onto the floor of the lake. During spring and summer, however, flows are sufficient to carry coarser materials out into the lake where they settle.

This process produces distinct layers, each representing one year of sediment accumulation. One can count the individual layers, the *varves*, to create a calendar of Lake Hitchcock's lifespan, about 4,100 years. The distribution of material in these ancient deltas can also tell a great deal about velocity and size of the streams that formed the delta. From this one may infer the weather conditions prevailing at the time the delta was formed.

In some places, near the ice margin or adjacent to deltas, the amount of rock "flour" released by the melting glacier was sufficient to produce varves that are up to one meter thick. In a field near our house, Colonel Ebenezer Green, who arrived in the valley in 1761, used a clay varve for his brickyard. This clay is about 75 feet above the current Connecticut River water level. The varve, once on the bottom of Lake Hitchcock, then baked in the kilns of Colonel Green, is now the red brick of the classic houses in our neighborhood.

When the dam of glaciated debris at Middletown, Connecticut eroded there must have been dramatic downstream events. However, when compared to the glacier's pushing the substance of Long Island,

100

Cape Cod, Martha's Vineyard and Nantucket into place, Lake Hitchcock's role in the remodeling of New England seems unimpressive.

Today as I paddle my canoe along the narrow channel of the Connecticut River as it traverses the very bottom of the ancient lake I wonder about the geologic history of other places I have visited by canoe.

After paddling the Wild and Scenic portion of the Missouri from Fort Benton Montana, the shuttle driver pointed out an interesting cliff in the distance. During the last ice age, a glacier forced the Missouri River far south toward the Big Belt Mountains. This escarpment was what was left of a falls the Missouri poured over in this ancient channel.

If you take the flight from Salt Lake City to Idaho Falls on your way to run the Middle Fork of the Salmon, keep your eyes peeled on the ground. Here, about 16,800 years ago, landlocked Lake Bonneville filled the Salt Lake Basin. When it had reached almost the size of Lake Michigan it slopped over its shore at Red Rock Pass. The result was catastrophic. The outlet it cut away was through relatively soft material and the lake dropped about 375 feet fast; the flood was probably over in a month or two, the rest "trickled out" in one year. The magnitude of that flood is not apparent to the untrained eye at ground level, but from five miles up, the evidence of the surge is obvious. Put yourself in that ancient floodscape with a canoe!

Jean and I had a lesson in the force of ancient rivers when we canoed the Kopka River in Ontario. The last major rapid on the river drops down into a small pond before completing the rest of its drop in a second cataract. The portage down to this pond includes a section with fixed rope—that should give one a fair understanding of the topography.

We and two friends canoed down to the south end of this pond, drifting up against a sheer cliff so large that it left us feeling insignificant. Then it dawned upon us. This "pond" was really a huge plunge pool at the bottom of what had been a falls when the flow volume was perhaps

100 times larger than the present river. As the ice sheet melted, the river had flowed over this precipice. We looked far up the cliff to the verge and imagined the force of the falls.

It is easy to identify water-worn rocks by their smooth surfaces. For the first few decades of my life I imagined the slow process by which the rocks were made smooth, water-borne abrasives slowly grinding away at the surface, and floods occasionally flipping up a new surface for abrasion. Considering the number of smooth rocks in the world, I marveled at the amount of work performed in this manner. It made the rivers I canoed seem very old.

Then one day my view of making smooth rocks was abruptly changed. Jean and I had left Pulpit Rock on the South Nahanni River in heavy rain that became a deluge as the day progressed. Soon every gully on the mountain slopes was belching muddy water into the river, cascades came off the high cliffs, and furious rain drops pocked the river in front of us. We came upon what was ordinarily a small steep stream coming down from the hills to enter the Nahanni on the right. Now it was in full flood. As we grew nearer I could hear a sound similar to what one might hear behind the pin setters in a large bowling alley—big resonant things being banged together. It turned out that the flooded creek was filled with head-sized boulders moving with the flow. They smashed into the banks, themselves, and anything that got in the way and poured out into the Nahanni. I will not forget that sound.

What Jean and I had witnessed was an extraordinary rock polisher, and suddenly all those rounded rocks we had seen in the past didn't have to be quite so ancient in order to explain their shape. In fact, studies of the smooth "melon gravel" (average boulder diameter of three feet but ranging to ten feet) found in the path of the Lake Bonneville flood have revealed that they were formed within the first few miles after being ripped free from the upstream basalt layer. Some deposits of these boulders are 300 feet thick, and it is likely that the flood accomplished all this work within a few weeks after the first water lapped over the rim at Red Rock Pass. The earth's remodeling can be slow or fast.

Although geologic and climate history can be inferred from counting and characterizing the year by year record embedded in glacial varves, helpful information also comes from other records. A story of the last ice age and its climate is recorded in ice itself. Based upon the studies of cores taken from the Greenland ice cap which provide an annual record of snowfall and water temperatures going back 115,000 years, it is now quite certain that climate change may occur rapidly. The ice record, including isotopic studies of oxygen in the annual winter/summer layers, shows that the climate of the earth for the last 15,000 years has been favorable for the development of the complex civilization that we currently enjoy.

But if we are to believe the ice record, it is a mistake to assume that the earth will consistently offer a climate so favorable for the operation of our kind of society. How long the current benign phase of climate will last is uncertain, but the record indicates that such periods do not usually persist much longer than the one we are presently in. Whether the activities of man will promote or forestall such a change is also open to debate. The best minds suggest that man should be prudent in how he tinkers with climate. A good time to think about such matters is when one sits in a gently rocking canoe in a plunge pool looking up at what was once an ancient falls. In view of what could be coming down river in the future, prudence seems like a good way to go.

In terms of the earth's budget for heat, it is the oceans that really matter, not the air temperature. Water from retreating glaciers and thinning ice caps has already increased the amount of fresh water entering the North Atlantic enough to change the salinity of this portion of the sea. Some oceanographers hypothesize that this change could shut down the Gulf Stream. Things then get very interesting. (First, sell your real estate in northern Europe; potatoes won't grow there any more.) Because the Gulf Stream acts as a pump transferring heat from the equator to the north, we can expect more deserts in the tropics and after a time, more ice in the north. Isn't it interesting how global warming could possibly speed the arrival of the next ice age?

Should we be concerned about such matters? After all, a human lifetime measured on the geologic scale is brief. Many are content to enjoy life to its fullest, to let life's pleasures reign without much thought about the future. But man has been given a brain that is unique among animals with respect to its ability to speculate about the future. Not to exercise it for this purpose is slothful. Put yourself in a mood to witness the full fury of the Kopka falls, or the Bonneville flood. When you are done with these events then imagine yourself in a coastal village on the ancient Black Sea when the Mediterranean came over its brim.

Think about the cold breeze that will coast down off the growling ice sheet to chill the bones of those who await better weather—those living without the agricultural bounty we take for granted. Imagine the courage, the conviction, it will take for successive generations to preserve and to pass along an inventory of human knowledge when surviving the next day or week may be continually in doubt.

For those who cannot or will not believe that the earth's climate will change, or who feel that when it does, man will come up with a technical fix for it, I wish you pleasant dreams. For my part I'm going to continue to hold the opinion that perpetuity, when used in the context of conservation easements, will be over when the edge of the next ice sheet crosses the Canadian border.

Companions

THE COUPLE SHOULD HAVE FIT RIGHT IN. They had paddled many of the rivers the rest of us had traveled. Their equipment was in good shape, and their judgment about what rapids could and could not be run was fine. But before the first day was up the rest of us on the trip were unhappy with them and we had another six days to go.

They argued. Insults flew between them. The climate produced by their spiteful words spilled over onto the otherwise happy members of the group. It poisoned the great outdoors. It started at the put in and reached its peak in the rapids. Jean and I had heard from old timers that having a husband and wife in a tandem canoe was a good step on the pathway to divorce. We paid no attention to it until this trip, however. As we listened to this couple belittle each other over every minor deviation from perfection, we could understand what the old timers were talking about. It was loud. It grated. It was a cancerous pain. We would have settled for anything to drown out the bickering.

The first evening on our Quebec river trip the woman made dessert for us, a huge pot of chemically green synthetic pistachio pudding, lots of cornstarch and no flavor. It didn't sell. A friend and I took the bowl scrapings plus the large amount left in the pot a quarter of a mile back into the woods. We found a couple of boulders with a crack between them that disappeared into darkness. As we emptied a green torrent of pudding into the void we experienced the first joy of the day.

For the next six days when I felt abused by what I heard, I thought about how we treated the pudding, and it made me feel better. At last the trip was over. The couple was not invited to go with us again.

The dynamics of a group is a critical factor in whether an outdoor adventure is fun and safe. Even with the most careful vetting of candidates for a trip, mistakes can be made, but the risk of such mistakes can be minimized. As we met other paddlers on day trips and friendships developed Jean and I could usually predict how these new friends would meld with our old ones on a longer trip. Usually, we tried to have trip participants meet before the trip so that some bonding could occur before the stress of the departure was encountered.

One of the differences between an outfitter trip and a private trip is that those participating in the private trip have not been randomly selected. On the other hand, when a participant spoils an outfitter led trip, the hurt is not as severe. It was the outfitter, not one of the trippers who goofed in selecting the team, and the outfitter often is the person who must deal with the client's offenses.

But even when chance throws a group of people together there may still be a perfect outcome. A few years ago I was hiking alone near Moab, Utah. As the day progressed the wind grew steadily and I wondered whether it was advisable to continue. Ahead of me, the trail rose onto a lengthy spine of smooth red rock and I chose to follow it. The spine grew higher with more exposure on both sides, and soon the wind threatened to blow me off. Nearby were three other hikers crouching low and moving slowly. I caught up with them and it was clear that they, too, shared my concern. We moved on a bit and then spotted a route off the spine to a parallel route that lay in the shelter of the rock. However, while we could jump from the overhang at the bottom of the spine to the ground below, we might not be able to climb back up once we were down. Nor was it clear that if we took the jump that we had a feasible route to rejoin the trail further along. We might have to retrace our steps and get back up on the spine.

If the four of us stuck together, however, and we had to retrace, it was likely that three of us could lift and boost at least one person to hand holds above the overhang. That person could spring us from the trap, if necessary. So we made a bargain: we would stick together.

As it turned out, we were able to return to the trail further on. Over the next couple of hours the wind subsided so that we no longer had to shout to communicate. We could also shake some of the wind-driven sand from our clothes and hair. We ate lunch and hiked on together. As we chatted, we found out that we were a cancer center director, a single mother who was in drug rehab following a bad auto accident, a biologist in a small college who was not certain what his life would hold, and a wealthy industrialist with strong conservative views. We had been bound together as tightly as any group I have ever traveled with and it was natural for us to continue our hike together.

There are those who question the value of helping others. They feel that "survival of the fittest" is the way humans evolved and that we should not let altruism interfere with that process. I agree with the opposite position taken by those who argue that the ability to cooperate with other humans is an important selective factor in the survival of our species. In summary this argument goes, "If you are going to hunt a mammoth with a spear, you should take some friends with you and make certain they have spears, too."

Here is another test of that premise. There were six of us in three canoes. After we passed the creek that entered the South Nahanni—the one where we heard the bowling-pin crashes as water-driven boulders spewed into the river—we started to look for a campsite. Originally we had planned to camp on the alluvial fan of Prairie Creek. We pulled ashore in the driving rain and found a poor site amongst low spruces a few feet above the surrounding sandy delta. It would have seemed a decent site had we not so recently observed that other creek out of control.

So we set off again continuing downstream near the right bank where the map displayed a "sign-in station," presumably a building. We coasted along, looking for a cut in the nearly vertical river bank. As we went the bank grew higher. After a half mile, we found a rustic ladder leaning against the steep bank, its top step at the level of the ground on top. At the bottom of the bank there was a beach about 10 feet wide upon which we landed.

Set back from the bank perhaps 75 feet was the sign-in station, possibly a former ranger station, a deteriorated building about 15 feet square. It lacked a cover for the chimney hole, and the roof was in poor shape with rotting eves and breaks in the asphalt roll roofing.

We lifted our gear up the ladder and set up camp amongst some large spruce trees near the top of the bank. Soon we had a tarp up and dinner cooking. There were a number of good tent sites, a picnic table, and shelter was provided by the cabin despite its leaky roof. I put a rock marker on the beach at the water line and we tied the canoes next to the base of the ladder about three feet above the river.

After dinner we had a look around the area. The view inside the cabin made up for its dreary exterior. Fastened to the wall or hung from lines that crossed the interior were several hundred miniature wood paddles. These had been carved and then signed by paddlers from all over the world who had then left them as evidence of their passage. Jean and I found paddles as well as entries in the log-book from a number of our paddling friends.

Behind the cabin was a food cache supported by a triangle of cross bars attached high on three large spruce trees. The trees had been wrapped in metal roofing to discourage climbing bears and the ladder that we had found served a dual purpose, providing access to the river and, when relocated, to the cache.

We went to bed early, with the rain still falling, although not as hard as earlier. Upstream the mountains were still lost in black storm clouds. I arose at 3:30AM and checked the canoes. My rock was submerged and the water was a foot and a half from one of the boats. A piece of the bank had given way, and the fallen earth covered parts of two canoes. I awoke Jeff and Chet. We hauled the canoes up the bank and put them close to the tents. As the water rose to the foot of the ladder we roped it to a tree but left its legs in the water in case a boater needed it for access. As the water rose further, we removed it.

About noon four young Canadian men in two canoes arrived at our campsite. While we were at Pulpit Rock two days earlier we had heard a substantial rock fall high on the canyon wall. It was likely that our newly arrived companions were the intemperate climbers who had set it off. The reserved way we greeted them upon their arrival reflected our concern about what kind of companions they would make at the campsite. The river now stood about 5 feet below the top of the bank.

From our vantage point we could look across the hundred yard wide river to the large alluvial fan of Prairie Creek. The narrow end of the fan extended more than half a mile back into the valley from which the creek emerged. The wide end of the fan lay stretched low and sandy along the far side of the river for a mile. We were reassured that for each foot the river rose, more of the fan was covered by the flood waters. As the river spread out, the volume could grow without affecting the water level as much on our side. Far up on the fan a huge log lay partly buried, the relic of a previous flood, and this served, along with the water level where the ladder had been, as a measure for us to assess the river volume.

By evening, the water level was four feet below the top of the bank and the tree hulk on the fan was surrounded by water. Jean and I turned in. Chet and Kathy watched the tree hulk depart at about 10:30PM. At

4AM I awoke the others after finding the river about to come over the top of the bank. The Prairie Creek fan was now completely covered by floodwater. Cracks had appeared several feet back from the top of the bank all along the river edge near our tents warning us that it was time to move the tents further from the riverbank. We also took down the tarp and moved it and the picnic table away from the river.

The Nahanni was now making a mechanical hissing and humming sound that rose against the background crash of water produced by the large standing waves in mid-stream. Single trees as well clumps of five or more trees passed. Some of these flipped about unpredictably, dunking and thrashing their tops. A few oil drums also floated by along with a Styrofoam float. Then an impressive black plastic box hove into sight; the composting toilet and its contents from the Pulpit Rock campsite was sailing past.

Our four Canadian campmates were also impressed by the cracks in the riverbank near their tents and they too decided to move away from the bank. Neil, one of the Canadians, had gone south into the woods behind the camp the night before in search of a cleaner water source. Now he came to tell us that about a hundred yards south there was slightly higher ground. Beyond this there was some lower ground before the land rose on a hill about half a mile further on.

Now a large spruce tree from our campsite leaned toward the river and plunged in taking a swath of river bank with it. At least there were now ten of us facing the flood. An extra four people to contribute their ideas and their muscle to our common problem. We came up with a plan.

I asked Neil if he would mark a trail across the brush and fallen trees—the aftermath of an old forest fire—that lay between us and the hill. The rest of us reinforced the bear cache and put all our gear on it except for what would be needed for a two day bivouac. We carried the canoes back a hundred feet from the river and tied them to sturdy spruce trees after clearing enough brush so that they had room to weathervane in the flood waters should the flood reach them.

Soon Neil returned. He reported that there was water flowing in a slough between us and the hill but that we could probably get across it. There were some delays in getting all our gear sorted out but soon we were able to move out with our packs through the burned over area. By the time we reached the slough, however, the water was too high to cross safely. A hillside camp was out of the question. We found a possible campsite on ground about a foot higher than the water in the slough, but decided to return to our original camp. Even the prospect of a night crowded together on the bear cache seemed better than what we saw here.

Upon our return, we found several newly arrived canoes and many more people near the cabin. Nick Parks and his contingent of students from Britain had arrived from Pulpit Rock. They had packed up in the middle of the night when the flood-water came over the campground there. Nick had linked their canoes together to make a raft. This diminished the risk of upset in the boils and when crossing eddy lines during their harrowing overnight paddle. The students were safe but shaken by their experience.

By now the water was over the top of the bank and had flowed half way up the path leading to the cabin. There was precious little ground remaining on which to accommodate the new arrivals. The spruces at the top of the bank continued to topple as the current tore away their underpinnings. Off they went surrounded by other flotsam. We imagined the tangle of trees and debris we would find lodged at some point downstream.

And then late in the afternoon the sun appeared and the water on the path to the cabin stopped its forward progress. Twenty or perhaps 25 of us now tried to figure out how to camp on this small swatch of high ground. We were linked by our common predicament and understood the common need. With this as background we jammed the tents into the space available while we traded stories with our new companions about our failed trip to the hill and listened to student tales of a night paddle on the hissing river.

Jean and I retired early that evening. The soft conversations connecting the various closely pitched tents were suddenly interrupted by a shout from the river.

"Take a rope!"

There was a scramble. Someone came up with the rope and was able to snub it around a tree. By now there were several to help. The rope held and two large rafts loaded with passengers swung their ponderous bulk into the bank downstream in a shower of broken vegetation and muddy earth. In a stroke, the number of people on the campsite was doubled. Each year about 750 people travel some or all of the South Nahanni River. Our one campsite now held about 50 of them.

The raft guides were Canadian. The passengers were from France. It was clear that the trip they were on was not the one described in their travel brochure. Jean practiced her French, speaking with a distinguished looking man who had fallen out of the raft when it encountered large waves. Though rescued, he was cold, wet, hungry and unhappy. His son had invited him to go on the trip. "He is trying to kill me!"

So on into the evening the raft guides fed the passengers and tried to get them settled down. It was sort of a "second sitting" at the sign-in cabin restaurant. And later, here and there, the Frenchmen found places to sleep. I remember thinking how clever Jean and I had been to place our tent against a large log where it would be hard for someone to step on it in the night. And during the night the water began its long creep back down the bank.

By the time a beautiful morning had dawned, the water had receded several feet. Spirits were high and we could assess what had happened. The trees on which we had first hung our tarp, about 10 feet back from the top of the bank, were gone. So were the trees around them. One large tree lay in the water parallel to the bank, its roots trapped by the roots of others still standing above. Our canoes were still tied back in the woods. The water had not floated them. The Prairie Creek alluvial fan was still under water. The debris coming down stream had decreased. There were still standing waves in the river.

One of the raft guides led a group of us along the sodden riverbank a half-mile to a patrol cabin used by the Nahanni wardens. It was locked and vacant but the guide had a key. He used the radio there to let his company know that all his clients were safe. By the time we returned the water had dropped another foot. The ten "old hands," six of us and our four Canadian friends, watched the river carefully as it fell. Around noon our decision to embark was made simultaneously. We placed the canoes against the muddy bank amidst the tangle of tree roots and loaded gear along with showers of crumbling earth that fell into the canoes each time the bank was bumped.

While the others loaded, I inspected the tree roots next to the canoe and I thought of bark canoes laced together with such roots like the one I had seen at Camp Vermilion so many years before. I had always imagined that the roots were gathered by pulling them one root at a time from a stubborn stream bank. After seeing this flood, I suspect that the native in search of spruce roots awaits a big flood and collects enough roots for a hundred canoes all at once.

At last the ten of us were all loaded. We were in good spirits and on the water again under clear skies. Our convoy of five canoes sped downstream leaving the crowded campsite behind. Those who were left behind could use the space and we could use the freedom. For a time all five canoes remained close together: The four young Canadians kept close watch on us, for by now they were referring to us as their "parents." But eventually, when they saw that we were capable of paddling big water and enjoying the trip through it, they let their stronger muscles speed them on and from the distance they waved good-bye.

We had a fast and exciting trip through the canyon and camped at Kraus Hot Springs after paddling 30 miles. We were six again. Old friends with predictable behaviors. We understood enough about each other to make things easy. After dinner we enlarged the hot spring tub that had been scooped out of the sand and pebbles. While we were soaking we knew the flood water was now sweeping on far ahead of us. The threat was over. As the group relaxed in the water, an estrogen patch floated to the surface. We didn't ask whose it was. We didn't have to explain to strangers that hot water was bad for adhesives. We were just old friends on a canoe trip.

When we took the canoes out at Blackstone Landing Provincial Park several days later there was a rumpled note awaiting us. It was from the four Canadians. Its address: "To Our American Parents." The last two words were double underlined.

Companions

Calories, the Point Where Physics and Nutrition Meet

THOSE OF YOU WITH INQUIRING MINDS have probably already discovered that long-grained rice will burn just fine in your pellet stove. (The stove will also make heat if you feed it corn but avoid popcorn if you want a quiet evening.) This conversion of food to heat is what lies behind successful expedition meal planning.

The first genius America produced, Benjamin Thompson (later known as Count Rumford of fireplace fame), once watched a horse powered drill as it worked its way down into an iron casting to make the bore of a cannon. In this process the drill bit and the cannon barrel became hot. He deduced that the amount of work done by the horse in boring the hole was directly related to how hot the casting became when drilled. His calculations relating the heat produced to the energy consumed were remarkably accurate by today's standard.

Now you have all the basic knowledge that is necessary to become the nutritionist for an extended canoe trip. Food can burn and put out heat, or food may be converted to energy and used to perform work. It also may be converted to storage forms of chemical energy. Heat may be used to perform work and work will produce heat. The two are interconvertible. Heat is measured in calories, the amount of heat required to warm a milliliter of water one degree Centigrade. In nutrition heat is measured in kilocalories, or a thousand calories; each kilocalorie is referred to as one capitalized Calorie.

You can find out how many Calories are in food by setting fire to it and then capturing and measuring the heat produced. To do this accurately is troublesome, but it has been done enough so that we know a gram of carbohydrate generates four Calories when burned. Burning a gram of Protein also puts out four Calories. A gram of fat, however, generates nine Calories when burned.

One thousand grams—a kilogram (or 2.2 pounds)—of carbohydrate or protein therefore delivers 4,000 Calories when burned, while a kilogram of fat yields 9,000 Calories under the same circumstances.

The requirement that food packaging contain a "Nutrition Facts" label has become very helpful to those who must plan expedition menus. These labels describe a "serving" in grams and state the weight in grams of the amount of carbohydrate, protein, and fat in that serving. It also specifies how many Calories are in a "serving." Doing some math you will find the number of Calories that you calculate from the number of grams of carbohydrate, protein and fat as stated on the label come to about the Calories per serving stated on the label. Slight differences are due to rounding off.

You should note that the "Nutrition Facts" label is based upon the number of calories in a serving for a person who is consuming 2,000 Calories per day. It is a mistake to assume that the "serving size" on the Nutrition Facts label is appropriate for everyone.

How would you find out how many calories people use as they perform various activities? By measuring oxygen consumption we have learned that a 65 kilogram (143 pound) male who is sleeping or resting quietly requires about 600 Calories in eight hours of sleep. A 55 kilogram (121pound) woman requires about 430 Calories for eight hours of rest or sleep. (In general, men have more muscle mass and women a bit more fat which is less active metabolically than muscle, and this explains the difference in the nominal basal metabolic rates given above.)

A "lily dipping" paddler is probably consuming 900 Calories in an eight hour trip. A motivated paddler consumes around 1,200 to 2,000 Calories in eight hours. A person paddling and wading a loaded boat upstream in cold rain while shivering a bit for eight hours might consume 2,500 to 3,000 Calories.

Cooking, chopping firewood, carrying gear, stuffing sleeping bags, slapping mosquitoes, standing around, and laughing at jokes for eight hours requires 800 to 1,800 Calories.

So on a wilderness canoe trip for a 24 hour day, a 65 kilogram person might expend a total of 600 Calories sleeping, 2,000 Calories paddling, and 1,500 Calories in miscellaneous activities or a Grand Total of 4,100 Calories.

The larger a person is, the more Calories they are going to require to get through the day, just as larger vehicles require more gas. Smaller people may spend more Calories per kilogram of body weight to maintain their body temperature when it is cold, however, so estimating Caloric needs is complicated. Photos of one expert canoeist Jean and I traveled with consistently show her sitting or resting while others stood. Although she is unaware of it, she has reduced her energy expenditure except where it counts, moving the paddle. She spends fewer calories than those of us who fidget. In fact, when the genes for obesity are finally all worked out, I predict that one will govern the tendency to fidget.

L et us now figure out how to feed a wilderness tripper who is expending 4,100 Calories per day. Because each gram of carbohydrate or protein when burned delivers four Calories we could feed that person 1,025 grams or about 2.2 pounds of carbohydrate and protein combined.

But a gram of fat delivers nine Calories. So we could feed the person about one pound of fat.

Of course a diet of pure carbohydrate, or protein, or fat is most unusual. A good recommendation is that no more than 30 percent of our Calories should come from fat, and most people eat a lot less protein than carbohydrate. Many expedition meal planners try to get the necessary calories into a food pack that weighs no more than two pounds (or 908 grams) per person per day. If that allotment contains 136 grams of fat, it delivers more than enough to feed a paddler burning 4,100 Calories per day.

One trip leader I know has insisted that the food pack for a six member party should weigh no more than ten pounds per day. If the diet of his paddlers derives no more than 30 percent of its calories from fat, and if his paddlers burn 4,100 Calories per day, his paddlers will lose weight. To avoid that, his diet should include 35 or 40 percent of the Calories coming from fat. This is not a bad thing. If you are working hard, and not gaining weight, taking your Calories from an increased percentage of dietary fat is not unreasonable. The fact that people who are losing weight on wilderness trips crave fat should tell us something.

As I look at the photos of the party that takes the ten pound per day food supply, it is clear that only one of them approximates the 65 kilogram weight that the above calculations are based upon. The rest of them weigh considerably more. From their trip reports it is also clear that they have encountered significant weight loss on a ration of 1.67 pounds of food per day. Weight loss may actually be a desirable outcome for some who take long canoe trips, but this should be acknowledged before setting out, not when a larger member of the party demands an increased share of the food at a time when the rest of the party is hungry.

Unfortunately, it is not as simple as I have made all this sound. Under the stress of an adventurous canoe trip, the participants may gain weight due to retention of fluid, lose weight because of dehydration, and change their metabolic rates as a result of disturbances in the normal level of various hormones. We have to consider other events that may occur on a canoe trip.

Jean and I both "hit the wall" one day. It was one of those times when paddling against the wind, you pick out a bush or rock on the shore and paddle for 10 or 15 minutes before checking to see if you have passed it. The wind was cold out of the northwest and the whitecaps splashed over us. Quite suddenly our paddle strokes became ineffective and we were lucky to come ashore behind a small point without swamping in the surf. Crouched out of the wind behind a rock, Jean tore open the wrapping on a pound of dates which vanished in a moment. Dates are an excellent source of glucose. An hour later we were again underway and the "wall" was only a memory.

Longtime Maine guide Alexandra Conover advocates keeping a 9 ounce packet of condensed mincemeat on hand in the emergency pack. This small box, a size that can easily be consumed by one person despite a label indicating that it contains 6 servings, will provide 900 calories, most of them from carbohydrate, and would help a person get through a cold night in the open.

But you have to plan for more than just emergencies. When the energy used is greater than the caloric intake for long periods, the body breaks down protein and burns the resulting amino acids. This happens along with the conversion of body fat to Calories. Thus, muscle wasting will be a factor in the weight loss that occurs in a person working for a long time in a severe Caloric deficit. Of course, the muscles are no longer hauling around as much fat, so that may be okay up to a point, and eventually more fat than protein is burned. By the time muscle wasting is advanced, however, you and your trip are in serious trouble. Eating enough protein, and thereby gaining amino acids for muscle preservation or reconstruction is important.

Even if sufficient Calories are present in the diet, people can still suffer from protein malnutrition. Humans can synthesize some of the amino acids for assembling protein, but eight amino acids must be obtained in the diet. These eight may be lacking in some food packs prepared for extended trips. Wheat flour contains less than the required amount of the amino acid lysine. Cornmeal contains too little lysine and tryptophan. Soybeans, however, contain adequate amounts of all of the eight amino acids that humans cannot synthesize. So do fresh or dried milk or eggs. Meat and fish, of course, contain all of the essential amino acids. Gelatin (Jell-O) does not. Make certain, if most of the Calories in the menu come from wheat or corn flour and fat, that the pack also includes dried meat, milk, egg or soybean protein (sometimes referred to by non-vegetarians as "mystery meat"). These sources of essential amino acids will prevent unnecessary muscle loss.

Brad Dimock in *There's this River…Grand Canyon Boatman Stories* describes a starving dog found in winter at the bottom of the Grand Canyon by some boatmen. It behaved so irrationally, intentionally lying upon the freezing aluminum raft decks, that the rafters concluded that the dog in its starvation had digested its brain. I don't believe that the brain is tapped for Calories under nutritional privation—it just seems this way. I know that as I get really hungry those around me appear to grow stupid. Starving people get selfish, paranoid, and sometimes murder. Talk about a spoiled trip…

Some other factors need to be mentioned. If you try to burn cabbage in your pellet stove, your stove will go out, even if the cabbage is finely diced. There is too much water in the cabbage. Once it is dry, the cabbage is mostly cellulose. Dry cellulose burns fine in air—that is what a wood fire is. But cellulose, wet or dry, cannot be digested and burned by humans. The Caloric values in Nutritional Fact labels represent only the Calories that are available for use in humans.

The nutrition labels provide information about Calories per serving and the "serving" may contain water in the product or as prepared. Don't weigh cooked oatmeal to calculate the number of Calories in oatmeal or expect to get 2,400 calories from a two pound loaf of bread. I have heard people complain that granola is heavy and not worth carrying on a trip. Assuming that the granola is chewed finely enough to render intestinal absorption efficient, a granola carbohydrate/gram gives the same number of Calories as any other carbohydrate/gram. Granola frequently contains nuts. Nuts may contain as much as 50 percent of their calories in fat (look at the oil floating on top of "old fashioned" peanut butter.) If the nuts come out intact in the feces, however, those Calories cannot be used for paddling (except in most unusual circumstances).

An ounce or two of couscous will make a large volume of carbohydrate when cooked, but the Calories contained in that pile will be limited to those in the small volume of uncooked couscous. A cook who provides a couscous meal to hungry paddlers should not be puzzled when they return a short time later, still hungry. The volume might initially satisfy them, but in the end it will be the Calories, not the volume, they need.

During the first few days of a diet in which Caloric intake is significantly increased, the gut lacks the ability to absorb the increased Calories. It is not a good idea to bed down for that first night out after eating a meal that leaves you struggling to digest it. By the end of a week, however, the gut has shifted gears and can easily deal with the increased caloric intake. It makes sense to provide meals with slowly increasing Caloric values during the first week of a trip. By the end of the week the tripper's appetite has increased along with his ability to absorb the increased Calories and both are happy.

To those packing the food for a trip, volume is an important consideration. It is possible to cram a lot of Calories into a very small volume. I remember hearing about a tripper who simply ate a quarter of a pound of butter (1,026 Calories) each day to supplement his diet. A person who really enjoyed butter might achieve 4,100 Calories/day by eating a pound of butter! Imagine—a very compact food pack for 25 days weighing only 25 pounds! Make sure it is not left in the sun, though.

I have also heard of a person who spent a year on a diet so low in fiber and residue that he did not have a bowel movement for the entire time. He apparently remained completely healthy. Stressed as they prepare for departure and dehydrated during travel to the departure point, some trippers may become constipated. Mentioning the aforesaid low fiber experiment to those in this momentary distress however will not be helpful. Knowledgeable trip meal planners often provide a first meal that is loaded with fiber and which "sets it right" in short order. Think beans!

I've neglected vitamins in this discussion because they have nothing to do with Calories or physics. Don't worry about vitamins. There is plenty of B vitamin complex in the enriched flour or in the whole grains you packed. If you take along or harvest any fresh fruit, or use artificial fruit drinks that contain vitamin C, you are covered for vitamin C. There is also plenty of vitamin A in your diet if you have carrots or tomato-based meals of any sort. Unless you spend all the time in the dark, the action of sun on your skin produces vitamin D. If you are still worried about vitamins take one hexavitamin U.S.P. per day. The contents of the pill will be peed out on the landscape but you will feel "in balance" or "in control" and I wouldn't want you to feel otherwise.

A completely different approach to canoe trip meal planning is possible, but takes time and experience to develop. This method simply relies upon the volume of food packs to define food consumption. The paddlers select items from a supermarket and put them in the pack until it is full. Then they paddle. They catch fish, eat berries, gain or lose weight according to their mood and desires. When the pack is half empty, they head for home. This method, with the exception of the supermarket, is how hunter-gatherer tribes have fed themselves on trips for thousands of years. I hasten to point out that this method is only for people who, once turned, plan to retrace their route to their starting point. For those of you who set forth toward distant objectives across unknown country and who may find a long, almost dry river to negotiate along the way, I suggest that you put more peanut butter in the wanigan.

Coppermine: Six Dimensions

July 4, 1999:

FROM THE FLOAT PLANE WINDOW after landing on Point Lake in the Northwest Territories I could see that the water was high. A willow bush clinging to the rocky shore where we were to unload was two and a half feet below the water level. As that bush came into view my thoughts flicked to a passage written for the Accident Notes section of *Appalachia* by Gene Daniell in June of 1999:

> "Regular readers of these pages will be familiar with this writer's obsession with the schedule-generated accident—the error of judgement made because people have plans for the hike itself or commitments in the outside world that lure them into seeing things the way they want them to be instead of the way they really are."

I then returned to the job of getting myself and gear out of the plane. While the pilots moved stuff from the plane onto the float, we formed a baggage brigade and passed it from one to the next until in a few minutes it was all up high on several wide ledges. There were eight of us, all old friends from previous long trips. Chet, a retired engineer who once was once a part of the design team for a bomber powered by a nuclear reactor, and his wife, Kathie, contributed years of whitewater

129

paddling expertise. Jeff, an engineer who travels with a GPS and electronic thermometers, also carried a two way radio on this trip. His wife, Reed, is a potter and imperturbable paddler. Bruce and Laurie, the youngest members of the group, had the most experience on far northern rivers and were faster than the GPS in putting us on the map. Jean kept our sourdough starter safe and I brought along the first aid kit that was never opened during the trip. The median age of the group was over 65 years.

Our four folding Pakboat canoes, 28 days of food, and the rest of our supplies made quite a pile. The pilot said softly, "Do you have your camera ready? I will make a pass." A few minutes later my camera caught the Twin Otter low and fast, its props stopped by the shutter, as it zipped by on its way back to Yellowknife. We were now committed.

Point Lake spread before us. Although our original plan had called for landing near Obstruction Rapid, where the Coppermine River enters Point Lake from Providence Lake, we were 15 miles further north. The pilots reported that the lake was covered with ice only a week before. The north wind had driven much of that ice to the south where it packed the area around Obstruction Rapid. To the west and north of us the lake was clear. The black clouds that had hovered over the ice-filled end of the lake were breaking up. We had sun. The air was clean with an occasional aromatic hint of Labrador Tea. The breeze was soft and cool making ripples, not waves, on the lake. There were no bugs! This was the kind of day one sees in cover photos on canoe magazines or advertisements for paddles, not raingear.

We assembled our four Pakboats, folding canoes that are made by Alv Elvestad in Enfield, New Hampshire. They were in four large duffel bags each weighing between 50 and 60 pounds. Selecting this type of boat for the trip had made it possible for eight of us to travel together. Otherwise the Twin Otter can carry only three rigid canoes and six passengers. The boats went together easily—three seventeen footers and one sixteen and a half foot. We reinforced each of the nylon catches connecting the aluminum framework, binding the crossing with wire-ties, and inflated the airbags along the sides. This tightened the vinyl covered polyester hull over the frame.

After lunch we loaded the canoes and headed down the lake. The fine weather, lack of wind, and sleek canoes despite their heavy loads made for easy traveling. We stopped for brief rest where a granite slab provided a convenient landing. Kathie immediately spotted the dorsal fin of a large lake trout cruising near the surface. As we peered down into the water we saw several others. I suggested that we might have trout for dinner and the group was willing to delay our departure for a few minutes while I fished. Finding the Mepps #3 spinner and setting up the rod took longer than catching two lovely trout and cleaning them. That night, poached, the fish was tougher than our pizza crust—but good. Fishing remained excellent throughout the trip. The fish remained tough until we adopted the mayonnaise frying method that we learned from a fisherman acquaintance in Alaska. (Coat the fillets with mayonnaise and drop onto a maximally heated non greased skillet. Cook for two or three minutes per side according to thickness of fillet.)

July 5:

During the night there were brief rain showers. Morning dawned on a placid lake and during the day we paddled under a dramatic skyscape. Virga, precipitation that evaporates before it reaches the ground, slanted down from the dark underbelly of numerous cumulus clouds that studded the otherwise blue sky. We coasted along on smooth water and avoided any problem with the weather until we were setting up camp that afternoon. Then there was a sudden rain squall that tried to blow Chet and Kathie's tent inside out. I assisted them in getting some guy lines out to the arctic birch and willow bushes while surf pounded the nearby shore.

Point Lake is a large lake, about 90 miles long with many large bays or arms that offer themselves to the strong winds of the north. Although we expected to be windbound on some days, the vehemence with which this squall arrived and the rapidity with which it dissipated startled me. As the spray from the dashing waves rained down on the nearby vegetation, I imagined the struggle we could have been having out in the whitecaps. The words of "White Squall," Stan Rogers' song about Lake Superior, came to mind:

> *I told that boy a hundred times not to take the lakes for granted.*
> *They go from calm to a hundred knots so fast they seem enchanted.*

Behind us, above Obstruction Rapids and Lake Providence, was another lake, Lac de Gras, even larger than Point Lake and below us lay two more, Red Rock and Rocknest. Together, these lakes constitute a reservoir more than 200 miles long and at times 30 miles wide which feeds the Coppermine. I wondered whether the willows on Lac de Gras were under water also. If so, we were riding a huge volume of water moving toward the exit from Rocknest Lake. Because of the great depth and width of Point Lake the movement of the water was imperceptible, but it nevertheless was moving and our efforts were carrying us inexorably to the point where the reduced depth and width of the channel would reveal motion. How would it be then, this motion? Smooth, with boils and whirlpools, the rapids drowned out? Or would it be tearing over boulders and slamming into steep walls? Would the outgoing ice have ground along the shore so that despite the high water the shoreline would be relatively free of brush—like the Saint John—or would the water be in the trees? Others must have been having some of these same thoughts, but no one spoke of them.

The sun set a bit after 11PM and rose at 2AM. During the twilight hours in between, I awoke. Cold. I pulled out the extra sleeping bag and draped it over us. I was glad that an earlier visitor to the Northwest had described how cold the summer was and that we had included an extra layer of warmth.

July 6:

We awoke early to find heavy frost on the canoe. The air temperature was 23 degrees Fahrenheit. The lake was so cold that no mist was rising. The sun warmed us at breakfast. On a cold morning Jean and I like to get moving early, so we packed up in a hurry and left half an hour before the others.

The lake was placid. The sun shone down from its perch in the huge blue dome of arctic sky. There were just enough fair weather clouds to make it a proper sky. Within a couple of miles we entered a unique and mystical world. In the distance, the rocky shores and undulating tundra over the hills beyond was reflected perfectly from the flat water surface—an inverted image, but twin of the upright one before us. Above the shore was the sky dome, growing more brilliant as the sun gained height. And on the lake right in front of us that sky dome was also reflected. Soon we were paddling on a plane between these two worlds, our clue to the real world being the occasional view of the lake bottom passing by 20 to 30 feet below in water so clear that the torpedo shaped trout that sometimes went by appeared to be airborne.

If the rocks and sand we could see on the lake bottom was the real world, then where were we? We were moving silently between two imaginary three-dimensional worlds, one above, and one on the lake in front of us—six dimensions. We were in sight of a seventh dimension, the real one, the lake bottom, to which we could not—or dared not—go. I was disconnected. I wondered if this feeling was of the same sort that I might possibly have in the future—confused about which room was mine in an assisted living facility. It was not disturbing, but it was not entirely pleasant either.

The sun warmed us. We took off our heavy gear. And slowly the interface of these two worlds, the space between the upright and inverted shorelines, began to dance as the cold air over the water began to warm. The narrow meeting of the true and reflected shoreline now became wider; growing until it became the equivalent of the Great Wall of China running along the lakefront. Reflected light from patches of snow reverberated, flashing with the intensity of strobe lights on a runway approach. We found our path blocked by islands and points that evaporated into nothingness as our canoe approached them.

I had heard of arctic mirages, of islands over the horizon that come into sight and disappear as the air becomes a lens that bends miles of light, but I never expected to participate in one.

We ate lunch on a rocky point just northwest of where a broken wooden rack once filled with drill cores spilled the cylinders onto the ground. A record of the underlying rock strata punched out by some mining company, they dated from the early 1990's. Up on Lac de Gras the first diamond mine is now in operation hauling out 18 million pounds of rock a day so that two pounds of diamonds can be sent to your local jeweler. If you want to see Point Lake as we saw it, it would be a good idea to go soon.

We should have crossed to the north shore before lunch. By the time we had eaten, a strong breeze from the northwest had begun and it freshened as we started our crossing. Unlike a rigid canoe, the Pakboats are flexible, able to bend into the waves. Instead of slamming their bows into steep waves, they snake along, undulating over the wave tops, making little commotion and staying quite dry. I was delighted to see that we maintained reasonable freeboard as the waves passed behind Jean's seat and flowed back toward the stern. Despite this advantage, however, making a crossing on a big lake with heavy loads in the canoe is serious business.

That evening as the tired paddlers settled into places on the rock that best suited their personal contours we entered that relaxed after-scalloped-potato frame of mind and watched as the cloud pattern changed to mare's tails and the wind gradually rotated to the south. "A bad sign," said Bruce. Someone noted that weather lore and food seemed to have displaced sex as the principal topic of discussion—that is what happens, I guess, when the average age of the party exceeds 65 years.

July 7:

The weather sign was correct. We awoke to a strong northeast wind, light rain, and pounding waves. In the lee of a rocky ledge we put a tarp over a rope that was secured at one end around a chock stone placed in a crevice at the ledge top. The headroom was low and the rain let up about the time we had got the tarp hung. Tarps are not very practical or useful in this country. There are few trees on which to support them and the winds during the storms are too strong.

After breakfast as the rain let up a bit, Jean and I walked up onto the hills behind the camp. We found Chet and Kathie up there. They pointed out the clumps of mountain azaleas in full bloom, their bright almost microscopic flowers brilliant even on this cloudy day. The spotted saxifrage was also in bloom as were the pea-like flowers of a small vetch. We sampled the alpine rosemary, and, as the wind began to drop, headed downhill to the camp.

We had a hasty lunch in the dying wind, but by the time the canoes were loaded the wind had returned, this time blowing against us, and we struggled up the shore. Just ahead of us was a crossing to the large island occupying much of the northwest end of Point Lake. Crossing over to it exposed us to a couple of miles of open water where four arms of the lake intersected. The arms had 5 to 15 miles of water on which the wind could work. We had no intention of canoeing this in a strong wind and called it a day after only a few miles of progress.

That evening the air cleared and the wind dropped. As this happened, the bugs, which up to this point had been only temporary nuisances or chronic mild irritation, became a problem. Above us on the slope was a sandbank that made for easy digging and was the destination of those seeking a toilet. It was also in slack air and home to swarms of black flies. Later, in the security of our tent, we observed the aftermath. Dozens of crushed black flies fell out of our bloody underwear as we prepared for bed.

July 8:

Morning arrived at 2AM through heavy clouds. We arose at 5:30AM and paddled off under a gray sky. The gentle breeze raised only small ripples. We made the crossing in good time, moving swiftly on smooth water and under a light rain. The shore of the large island now lay to our left and we were able to cross from point to point along it with no wind threat from the large bays along its north side.

Later in the day, the sun came out and once more we had a fine crop of cumulus in the sky. Reed directed our gaze toward a "pornographic cloud."

Indeed, there it was, a puffball of a cloud with a huge phallus extending from it. The more inhibited members of the group interpreted the cloud pattern as a "teddy bear" which, of course led to additional discussion as to what the teddy bear might have been doing to himself. I regarded this discussion as evidence that our biological age was less than our numerical age—perhaps a lot less.

That evening we had a good dinner, the wind keeping the flies under control, but later when it died, they were troublesome. When I washed up that evening, I found blood-filled black flies still alive inside my pants from the exposure that morning. Jean and I had experienced flies worse than this only once, in northern Quebec. The others, with more experience in the Northwest Territories than us, felt that the bugs were the worst they had ever encountered. High water equals lots of black flies.

July 9:

We left the island shore and under a clear sky and with increasing wind, crossed over to the north shore of the mainland. We completed the crossing as whitecaps appeared. Jeff's GPS showed that we had covered 1.2 miles in one hour of hard paddling. This is what the day was going to be like. We pressed on for a bit against increasing wind before landing for an extended rest and lunch. This provided the opportunity to climb to the height of land where we obtained a good view of the country to the north. Below us a maze of caribou trails was imposed upon the dwarf birch and willows. In the distance, beyond the island on a bay of the south shore, we could see several buildings of an outfitter camp. The view through binoculars failed to reveal any sign of activity. Below us to the northwest was a small lake and we speculated about outwitting the wind by portaging and lake hopping over the isthmus separating Point Lake from Red Rock Lake. We decided against trying it for it would have been a long portage.

As we moved north and west down Point Lake a few spruce started to appear. Indeed, the map shows some large areas of green (denoting forest) near the outlet of the lake. Perhaps the wind moves the ice out of this part of the lake often enough and early enough so that the climate at this end of the lake has just enough warm days for the spruce to survive. It certainly is a borderline situation. Bruce demonstrated this by pointing out that many of the spruce had a "mop head." In this configuration the tree displays a bushy base about 12 to 18 inches high from which a nearly naked pole rises for a foot or more, followed by the resumption of branches above the naked area. The healthy appearing base exists because during the winter the snow cover protects it. The bare stem results when the leader on the tree grows above the snow cover. The side branches are then subjected to the full blast of the wind and the abrasive effect of the layer of wind driven snow which is most pronounced just above the surface of the snow pack. These die as a result of this blasting, but if the leader has received sufficient nourishment from the base of the tree it may struggle upwards despite the loss of branches below it. Finally, the leader reaches a level above the worst of the abrasive blowing snow and the side branches now survive, thereby creating the head of the "mop."

Returning to the canoes, we convinced ourselves that the wind had dropped a bit, but this proved to be wishful thinking. We struggled up the lake past a couple of additional points and called it quits.

July 10:

For several days we had discussed getting started earlier to avoid the wind that was usually stronger from noon until evening. After our experience of July 9, we resolved to get moving early. The next day I woke people with the following: "Good morning. It is four AM. The wind direction is unchanged, but the intensity has diminished. There are no white caps or squalls. The sky is almost cloudless blue. The temperature is in the low forties."

We got our early start and reeled off two and a half miles in the first hour against a slowly rising wind. We heard and then saw a peregrine falcon on the rock cliffs and watched as it circled away and then returned. By 9:15 we were at the end of Point Lake. Here we found a low shoreline on both sides of the narrows. On the left was a large metal building with no signs of activity and further along a smaller metal building the size of an outhouse supporting a small antenna which had been blown loose. I wondered whether it might be an automated weather station. We found ourselves in a brisk current as the river course narrowed and slid down through a long S turn in gentle waves. I was especially interested in the water level here in view of our earlier observations on Point Lake. As we examined the vegetation it was clear that my earlier observation of the water level was too conservative. The willow bushes were standing in at least 3 to 4 feet of water.

Soon we were slugging it out with the wind coming down Red Rock Lake. At least we had made some progress earlier before the wind came up. Ahead of us, Bruce and Laurie stopped paddling and pointed up the hill above the south shore 20 yards away. A white wolf was loping over the tundra and rock outcroppings, pausing from time to time to look over its shoulder at us. Eventually it topped the rise and disappeared. Despite the seaworthiness of our Pakboats, we were having a rough ride in the waves and no one tried to get a photo.

We tucked ourselves into what little shelter lay behind the shallow points and rested in an unattractive inlet as we struggled up the lake. Finally, we camped at a site of "convenience" since the shore beyond lacked any indication of good sites. We were a few feet above the water on a narrow strip of reasonably flat ground. Behind the site there were standing pools of water and the insects, once the wind had dropped, were formidable. Previous parties had stopped there. Some of the flat red shale that gives the lake its name had been thrust into the ground so that tent guy lines could be fastened to it.

July 11:

We got another early start departing in a light ripple and cruised down the lake making good time. On the right shore where a high cliff gives way to a nice point below and north of it, we found a cluster of buildings and a person standing on the dock. As we approached, he called out, "What'll it be?" The coffee drinkers were quick to respond. This is the camp of Max Ward, the bush pilot turned airline entrepreneur.

Beyond the dock there was an interesting collection of buildings. A couple of small cabins, some white-painted privies with fanciful rooflines, and a long gambrel roofed building with a view out over the docks were our first sighting. Beyond these there are two recently built homes that would fit right into a high quality suburban development.

Gary MacDonald was the man who had greeted us. "Did you hear the shot this morning?"

"No."

"I fired at a grizzly bear that swam the lake. Before I could get the gun out and load it, it had come ashore and had ripped the top off that locker over there."

"Did you hit it?"

"Oh no! I was only trying to scare it. I don't want to have to deal with a dead bear. I've got no way of handling it."

It then occurred to us that having to skin, butcher and clean up 500 pounds of dead bear in the middle of this camp of suburban houses would be a problem.

MacDonald informed us that the Ward family was spending the summer in Norway and that he was the only person here. He was doing some maintenance work and planned to do some caribou horn carving.

By noon we were at the outlet of Red Rock Lake where a brisk current and a few boils indicated the volume of water moving into Rocknest Lake. We ate lunch on a rocky outcrop at the juncture of the two. From this vantage point we observed two canoes as they came around the corner from Red Rock Lake. They were trim and well-equipped Ally canoes, a folding canoe made in Norway. Our friend Alv Elvestad imported Allys into the U.S. for several years before coming up with his Pakboat design. As they came near, I suggested that the occupants join us for lunch.

This proved to be a mistake, since the four Austrians in the boats interpreted this as our offer to provide them with lunch rather than to simply share the lunch site. The confusion was quickly cleared up, however, but in the future I will be more careful in how I phrase invitations. They were planning to complete their trip on the Coppermine on August 5th, seven days after we planned to finish our trip.

That afternoon as we moved down Rocknest Lake, I started to feel very sleepy. This was not good, since Jean had already stumbled a couple of times with her paddle. We could not both fall asleep at the same time! In order to prevent the loss of one or both of us from the canoe, we moved over to paddle alongside Chet and Kathie who were nearby. Soon we had a delightful discussion going and were wide awake. Suddenly, about 200 yards away near the west shore, there was a terrific rushing noise. A water spout was raised by a whirlwind that hustled it up 50 feet over the water for a bit and then collapsed leaving a spray that fell back down over the water. The sky was clear, there were no storm clouds near. I remembered the stories of people struck and killed by lightning on clear days, "out of the blue." Instinctively I reacted, preparing myself for a change in wind direction and within a moment it arrived—a gentle but cooler breeze 180 degrees off the existing wind direction pushed us down the lake for a minute before it faded and disappeared. That was it. No more. If we hadn't been paddling with Chet and Kathie I would have concluded that I had fallen asleep and that the whole thing was a dream.

We camped that night on a small island in Rocknest Lake. Rather than haul our gear up the slope Jean and I made do with a rough spot near the takeout. There were no ideal campsites and this one was no worse than average. We had covered 21 miles by 2:30PM—enough for one day. We bathed in the lake and washed some clothes. Once the skin is thoroughly chilled by the water, the bugs' infrared sensors fail to pick up signs of life. They have learned that there is no point trying to suck blood from a dead animal. By moving fast we got our clothes back on before the bugs realized that we were alive.

July 12:

We moved off at 8:00AM under cloudy skies and in light rain. As we twisted and turned as the lake gradually narrowed I imagined that I was able to sense a current. We passed an esker that came down to the lake on the left and we stopped briefly on a sandy beach just beyond it. Here we found fresh caribou tracks. A few hundred yards later we passed a forlorn cache set in some low spruce on the right. It was surrounded by fuel drums and looked like a miserable place to do anything other than fuel a plane.

Shortly thereafter we were in a brisk current. I noted that the brush covering a point on the right was well under water and paused for a moment to photograph the drowned shoreline. As I view the photo now, it confirms my mood of that morning. It is dark, under low clouds, the cold water courses through the underbrush. Landing on the shore below that point would be risky. The huge river boils along toward the first rapid.

The first rapid is shown as one line on the 1:250,000 map. The trip notes we were carrying with us show a rocky bar arising from river left which pushes the current to the right. Behind it is a large eddy. We pulled over to river right and clutched at willows, careful to avoid getting broadside to the current as we threaded our way to the drowned shore. The rocky bar was gone, submerged and replaced by boisterous white water. Below us on the right, the river flowed into and through a clump of spruce. At lower water these trees stood on a point, now submerged. We could not see around these trees to scout the water below. Bruce and

Laurie ferried across to the left shore and climbed a hill to scout the lower part of the rapid. While they did this we prepared lunch on a rocky flat where a fire ring indicated that others had visited this spot, perhaps to confront the same water conditions, The bugs were so numerous that it was difficult to eat. Lifting the bug nets briefly to stoke a cracker and cheese was hardly worth the effort. Soon a couple of people had ingested their hat straps along with the hastily gulped cracker. Hilarity reigned!

The decision was to bang down through the brush to a place just above the spruce covered point and to portage from there. My photo shows our canoe with its spray cover on crammed into the brush on that shoreline. It is not a nice place. The portage was not nice either. The trail was poor, crossed patches of loose boulders, and the high water sent rivulets ashore that trickled down the path. The rocks were slippery and we had not packed for efficient portaging. While carrying our canoe I stepped onto a slippery rock that suddenly tilted and nearly went down. Through the brush I spotted Kathie sitting down while wearing a pack frame to which a food barrel was strapped. She was not resting. Chet says that she hates portaging. The only serious injury that I have witnessed in my years of wilderness tripping occurred when a person slipped and fell on a portage trail. I worried about our portage today.

An unexpected portage tends to do interesting things to people. We had all figured that this first rapid would be runnable. Several of us had talked ourselves into it being runnable. When Bruce and Laurie told us that they would not run the corner around the spruce tree point because they could not see around it, and when, once below it they commented that the eddy line below it was likely to have upset us, we greeted this information with a healthy dose of disbelief. Confident of our abilities and fed up with lifting our gear over slippery rocks and embarking amidst tree trunks, the temptation was to "get out there and run it." Some of us paid too little attention to what lay below the point, what we would have to swim through in very cold water if we did upset, and the

143

formidable barriers confronting our potential rescuers. Furthermore, from just downstream we could pick up the low pulsating roll of the Class IV rapid we had been hearing while still on the lake several miles back. Despite this compelling rationale, the group was not happy. For the first time on the trip we were not of one opinion.

Finally, we reloaded the canoes in the midst of a flooded spruce grove and floated out into the current again. We passed some quick water where the Napatolik River enters from the right and zoomed on down to the top of the Class IV rapid about a mile below. We stopped and walked down the portage trail. This shoreline was remarkably clear of brush and on the right a series of eddies arising below several shallow points ran down it. A quick inspection suggested that sneaking along through these eddies would be a piece of cake. It is always a good idea, however, to inspect the entire rapid, and I'm glad we did. The sneak route on the right disappeared into a huge hole below a pourover about two thirds of the way down the rapid. To avoid this hole meant riding out in a sluice that ended in a catastrophic collision with the big stuff. A definite portage at this point, perhaps more below.

I climbed the side of the esker that ran along the right shore a few yards back from the river bank. At the top there were a few widely scattered spruce. There were fine campsites here with a view of the tumultuous water below. Suddenly, I felt tired and cold. The day was almost over.

I returned to the river and met the others. We decided to bring the boats down to where we could camp and prepare for the portage. Jean and I floated down the right shore doing a gentle backferry, keeping the stern tucked into the shore. While going around one point, I found that I could not draw the stern downstream enough to keep our ferry angle correct. Just for a moment we were headed toward the big stuff and making those on shore nervous. Then the stern pulled around and we were in the clear.

The photo I took that evening shows us cooking in a gentle rain. We are in heavy gear and it looks cold. I had decided that the climb to the top of the esker with our gear was worth it. We had a fine spot for the tent as a reward. It rained hard that night, but we were dry and snug. I slept soundly without thinking about the days ahead.

July 13:

Shortly after I crawled from the tent into the crisp morning air, Bruce and Laurie came over from their tent. They had not slept well, confiding that they had spent the night poring over the maps and trip reports and pondering what lay ahead. They suggested that we not take our tent down, since we would be spending some time at this site as we considered our options. Ordinarily, our tent is down and our gear is packed before breakfast, so this was a change.

In essence their concern was that we had taken two and a half hours for the portage of the first rapid. Because of the high water levels there could be 11 or more portages. If they all took the same amount of time, that would be 28 hours of portaging. Two or three days of portaging! I agreed that it was time to have a talk. The four of us clambered down off the esker to the river's edge where the others were camped.

Against a backdrop of the boisterous rapid behind us, we ate breakfast and discussed the future of our trip. Into this interchange went baggage that was at least as heavy as that weighting down our canoes. First, we had come a long way and had plunked down quite a few dollars to get to this place on the river. Second, half the people on the trip were 65 or older. While none of the group regarded this trip as their last hurrah, we were all mature enough to recognize that as we age, the opportunity to make trips such as this can vanish without much, if any, warning.

It didn't take us long to agree to one premise. If the river were in New England we would not paddle it at this water level. If it were not safe to paddle in New England, it certainly was not any safer now that we were in the wilderness 3,000 miles away. The water was cold. Although the shore line here was clear we could not be certain that this was the case down river. Lining rapids is always risky, especially if the river is high. We knew that lining was out of question for the several rapids with steep rock walls. Most of the eddies were in the trees or brush. Any swim would likely be a long one. Long enough to cause hypothermia. Getting a swamped canoe and swimmers ashore through the maze of inundated brush and trees would be a challenge.

Bruce ticked off the options:

We could go on down the river, taking time to be careful and probably arriving several days late at Kugluktuk, our planned takeout on the Arctic Ocean. We had three extra days of food with us and could stretch what we had further, if necessary.

We could go on down the river, past the next large rapid to a place where the map showed the river widening. We speculated that a plane might land on that part of the river to take us out if we decided not to go further. We were carrying a radio that was sufficiently powerful to communicate with the float plane base in Yellowknife. If the plane could not land at this place on the river, or if the radio didn't work, however, we would be committed to the rest of the river trip.

We could go back up the six miles of river we had just come down and call in a float plane to meet us at Rocknest Lake.

We also dealt with several uncertainties. The radio transmitter was untested. We didn't know how long the batteries that powered it would last. The further north we went, the further we were from Yellowknife and the weaker our signal would be. We knew that Gary MacDonald had a working radio back on Red Rock Lake and that we could get there, if our radio did not work. The place where the river became wider could be too shallow and rock-filled for a plane to land. In any case, it was too narrow to provide an alternative set down for the pilot to avoid a difficult cross wind landing. The rapids further down the river could be drowned out by the high water and we could have fewer portages than existed in the worst case scenario. However, they could be worse, and there might be a need for more, rather than fewer, portages.

Above all, it was important that we avoid injury to ourselves and our boats. In each of us, however, that premise entered the part of the brain that deals with self-preservation through a filter. I refer to this apparatus as the "belief filter." If a person really believes that they and their canoe will not be hurt—that they can make it through the challenge without undue risk—then there is no alarm. The filter is calibrated by past experiences, by the opinion of others, by what one ate for breakfast, and whether one is having a "good" or "bad" day. More than some of us can admit, that filter is calibrated by one's willingness to gamble with one's life.

When asked, I said I favored going further down river to the point where it widened. I quoted the optimistic widower who remarries: "a triumph of hope over experience." I said that I would rather go down the river I hadn't yet seen than go back up one that I had. Jean favored going back up to Rocknest Lake. She was not looking forward to longer portages that would be coming up. Even with the total weight of the food packs going down by 16 pounds a day, the group would still have a lot to carry.

Kathie got angry. Angry at the situation. Angry that others felt that the risk of proceeding downriver was too high. She was confident of her ability in the big water and suspected that there would be fewer, rather than more, portages. Chet sized up the situation as an engineer would. In addition, he saw the direction in which the majority was leaning and drifted comfortably into that position. Jeff was for the conservative option. Two years ago he had been with us on the big flood in the first canyon of the South Nahanni. While the rest of us had enjoyed the exhilarating ride, he had been most anxious, picturing what would happen to a swamped canoe and its passengers if they swam in the surf that pounded the canyon walls. Jeff was in favor of returning to Rocknest Lake. Reed, who ordinarily, I believe, is more willing to gamble with her life than Jeff, did not take a strong position, but opted for returning to Rocknest Lake.

Bruce and Laurie seemed to be more objective than the rest of us. They were better able to list the pros and cons of the options and to assign a score to them. Perhaps this is because they sensed that the only way to resolve the issue was to approach the emotional members of the group in this seemingly detached manner. However, there was never any question about what option they favored.

So the decision was to get out the transmitter to see if the float plane base could be reached and, if so, to request a pickup in six days at Rocknest Lake. We climbed onto the hill above the esker and strung out the 100-foot antenna between paddles held high over the rocks and tundra. Jeff and Laurie, crouched out of the wind in the lee of a boulder and reading from a script that contained the essential information, successfully raised the float plane base. Our message went through.

I had been against bringing the radio, feeling that it would intrude into the isolation characterizing such a trip. The temptation is great, once one has a communication device available, to use it to communicate. When one picks up the phone these days the voice that is heard may be from just up the road but sometimes it is from the top of some previously unclimbed mountain. I was afraid that once we had it with us, the radio would be used to convey birthday or anniversary greetings, or possibly to learn what the Dow Jones Industrial Average was doing. I also ran down the list of medical emergencies for which radio communication from this particular spot would make a life or death difference and found very few. However, when Jeff, the prime mover with respect to the radio, offered to put it in his pack and get it out only when the group reached a consensus that it was needed, I backed off. Now I was glad that he had carried the orange box and batteries for us.

So the decision was reached, cast in stone, since we could not be sure that the radio would work again. Several of us headed off to the height of land behind our camp. From here we could see our river heading west and finally disappearing north around a right hand bend. A river storming along with some big "V"s and standing waves. A river we would not take, at least for now.

July 14-19:

A fter the big decision everything becomes an epilogue. A very pleasant one, however. We worked our way back up the river, lining up along the rapid where we camped, working in our lightweight wet suits in morning air that registered 38 degrees. We had some neat moments when our canoes swung out into the current on 100 feet of rope that was just long enough to get us past a point. This was followed by some eddy hopping as we ascended the river. After ferrying to the other side we reached the bottom of the first rapid we had portaged on the way downriver. Here—on the other side from the one we had come down—we found a fine portage trail that frequently dipped, disappearing into deep water for a hundred feet before emerging again. We avoided the flooded portage trail and made a two-stage portage along caribou trails further back from the river. In contrast to the portage on the way downriver, the spirits of the group were good—everyone was pulling together.

We camped amidst a few spruce trees at a lovely spot high on a gravel hill overlooking the rapid. As I carried our pack up the gentle rise I spotted a small area covered with reindeer moss and lichen, surrounded by arctic birch into which several small stunted spruce had seeded. This garden was as fine as any of the Zen Temple gardens of Kyoto. It was hard for me to accept the idea that what I was seeing was the product of biology and randomness, not that of an artist. I put the pack down and got out the camera. Just then a cloud came over the sun so the photo is dull. The garden's brilliance will have to reside in my memory.

That evening, the four Austrians in the Ally canoes came past, lining and carrying along the flooded portage trail. I watched as they put their canoes in just above the inundated "rocky bar" and disappeared amidst the drowned brush around the corner. The next day we met Bill Layton, a canoeist well known for his many trips in this area. He and his paddling partner had started on Lac de Gras and were making good time. We spoke about river conditions for a bit. Chet and Kathie loaned Bill the hoops that supported their Black Feather spray cover. Layton's hoops had been left aboard the floatplane at Lac de Gras and he was going to need a means of supporting his spray cover in the rapids ahead.

After a lazy day at this campsite, we then paddled upriver once more, sometimes stalling out in tongues of water that were moving too fast for us, and at other times pulling ourselves upriver using the tops of bushes that were protruding from the water. We camped on an esker at the end of Rocknest Lake and spent the next couple of days exploring the lakeshore, eskers, and hills by foot and canoe.

The day of departure was cold and wet with a wind that strained the guy lines on the tent. Most of our gear packed, we had no foam pad to lie on in the tent. The arctic soil beneath us and the flapping of nylon under tension was a reminder of where we were and why. Then we heard the turbines of the Twin Otter and it was time to take down the tent. The trip was over.

When Bill Layton returned the spray cover hoops to Chet and Kathie he sent along this description of his trip:

Well we got off the river BUT not without some real hard days of BIG WATER. I think all round you people made the

right decision! We saw your story in the Yellowknife paper...
... We got down the river with a short portage at the second
rapid you turned back at, [We also portaged] Rocky Defile (although I feel it was paddleable), Muskox and at Bloody Falls.
When we got to Rocky Defile we caught up to another group
who had all decided to walk it and it was pouring rain and
cold..so we walked. Sandstone was real hard with a ferry
through criss cross 4 foot breaking waves! HARD class 3 and
one boat we met had a dude who paddles solo boat on the Ot-
tawa River and he almost got stuck in a hole as he set up for
his ferry way too low. He only got out cause it was a smiling
hole and blew him out the end!!! His wife was near hysteria
before he got to shore. I thought as I watched him we would
be doing a rescue for sure. Escape was easier for God sake! The
stretch from Sandstone to escape was all BIG with loads of ferrying from side to side through 2 to 3 foot stuff...and again
pouring rain and COLD all day. When we got to Kugluktuk
the RCMP told us about a group of Swedes just in front of us
who wrecked one boat and almost totaled another. They
limped in with 6 in two boats out of food and in real rough
shape...YIKES.

The people who passed us on the river while we were on our way
back up were younger and stronger. Our collective wisdom was
sound. The river was dangerous. It may take a life in the high water, but
it wasn't going to be one of ours.

Reentry By Canoe

AT THE FLOAT PLANE BASE the office manager went over to the large topographic map covering the wall behind the counter.

"We will shuttle your vehicles to the parking lot of the golf club located right here."

His finger wobbled over five miles of Quebec riverbank and finally descended, covering half a mile on the map. Something about the way the finger moved told us that he had never been to that golf course parking lot. We noted the location and stepped outside to load the Beaver for our flight to the put-in. Ten days later, we looked carefully at the mark on our topographic map.

"Do you see anything that looks like a golf course?"

"No, but it should be right there."

"Looks like a cow pasture to me. It's going to be hard going upstream if we have missed it."

"Better stop and check things out." We pulled in and Ralph walked up through the pasture eventually vanishing from our view over the hill. We waited.

Twenty minutes later he was back, with a smile on his face. "No house, just a road. I stopped a car and I tried to speak French with the driver. We had quite a conversation. Anyone know what 'golf' is in French? I think we should go down river."

A mile or two further along, we spotted a suction hose snaking down the bank into the river. It was connected to a large pump higher on the bank.

"Do golf courses need water?"

We scrambled up the bank. Now we could see the clubhouse and golf course that were invisible from the river. The vehicles were behind the club house. Everything was okay.

Although canoeists often spend 16 hours a day treading or sleeping on land, at the end of the trip it seems like landing and pulling the boats up for that last time puts them onto the solid phase with a jerk. On one of our trips a road joined the river and ran alongside it for the last several miles of the route. A car sped by raising a large dust cloud and disappeared around a bend. A moment later, for the first time in a couple of weeks I smelled gasoline. Although I was still paddling, my trip was over.

Sometimes more exciting opportunities present themselves. As our little flotilla came into the first signs of habitation on another river, we saw rooftops peeking over the top of the bank. They belonged to a row of houses that backed up to the top of the bank. We were paddling along quietly and we could hear a soft out-of-tune chorus of adult and children's voices singing "happy birthday to you" from one of the back yards. I chuckled at the idea—like pirates and with complete surprise in our favor, we could swarm over the bank with knives in our teeth and make off with the ice cream and cake. The children would never forget it!

Whatever the mood that prevails as the hard reality of the trip-end sinks in, confusion, depression, or slap-happy elation, eventually things smooth out.

The group photo has been taken, the team has broken up with promises of future meetings, sometimes kept and sometimes not. The gear has been cleaned and put away (which for some reason always goes faster than getting it out before the trip). Letters have been written, and photo duplicates have been mailed. And about the time when one's mood should be bottoming out, an amazing thing happens. A friend calls to announce that they are signing up for the permit lottery on a river that you have always been interested in running, would you like to come? Or would you be available to meet in Fort Liard in mid July? Or could they come and look over some maps of the Boundary Waters and Quetico that they know you have?

Then it all begins again. Planning, map reading, organizing gear, and packing stuff in the smallest, lightest, most rugged way possible. Otherwise dreary weeks fly by as one contemplates whether this route is feasible, and whose wanigan will be used for the condiments. We feel wonderful. I think it all goes back to the primitive brain. If motion gratifies certain ancient parts of our brain, we are also rewarded similarly for planning and for keeping things shipshape. You see, when early man set out on big water those who didn't like to do this kind of stuff didn't make it. The loose line, the frayed canvas, the spoiled food, the careless navigation did them in. Our genetics go back to those who made it. We do these things because in so doing, we are happy. It is just the way things are.

Old Canoes

FOR A CANOE TO BE OLD, someone has had to love it. Sure, there are those that are designed and constructed to resist abuse. There are photos in magazines that show them being tossed off tall buildings or being bruised by automobile bumpers. But how many bumpers will a canoe take? And if you really loved a canoe, would you throw it from a rooftop?

Hidden in the trees and bushes of innumerable shorelines, there are relics of unloved ones. Now I won't claim that every derelict that resides there was unloved, since some loved canoes die prematurely. But it is likely that the fragmented Grumman lying in the woods below the falls, the canoe that looks like a 50 pound bomb went off just in front of the bow paddler—that is peeled back on itself like two halves of an open pea pod—was unloved. At least not loved enough for the paddlers to tie it up before they went to scout the rapid. Or maybe the paddlers loved neither their canoe or themselves enough to make a prudent landing above the falls.

That strange white thing, looking like a slowly flapping and twisted sheet beneath the water, stuck in the boulders of the very first rapid of the route, was retrieved. "Hey, it's not cloth, it's Kevlar." There was enough of the deck left to show the name of the company that made the canoe. It took several of us to haul it out. We carried it back into the woods, putting the hulk next to the rusted ghost of an office typewriter abandoned when the logging company moved out. I saved one fragment of the hull that has since resided in the corner of my wanigan. It serves as a reminder that Kevlar, though strong, is not indestructible.

There are other canoes, beyond the lily pads in the weeds, down where the prevailing winds push floating detritus from the lake. Pick up a corner of old rib and plank, the canvas rips, and what remains in the hand is no stronger than a ripe mushroom. Behind the lakeside lean-to, up on some wobbly sawhorses, is another, this time with sponsons, a museum piece, but the canvas over the hull is coming off, the gunwales are black with rot. It is going, maybe already gone.

Why is this one here? It is at the end of a portage to a small lake, hidden back in the woods. Well-supported on a peeled log rack. Ah! That's it. The small lake has a camp on one of the islands. The people who own the camp cross the lake and take the portage to the large lake when they depart. They do this because the float plane can land to put them on their lake but it cannot take off from it with a load of passengers. Now, they haven't been to their camp in a couple of years, maybe more, and the canoe shows it. Soon it will be gone, and people will say, "It wasn't their best canoe, anyway."

One especially good way to arrange for the early death of a canoe is to have two people own it, or for the owner to let another person use it on indefinite loan. That is how my brother's Old Town wood/canvas got a hole bored through the stern planking. "Wanted to be able to get the water out of it," said the person who had planned to insert a cork in the hole after the water had drained.

For a canoe to last a really long time, I think it has to demand a bit of attention from its owner. An owner who likes the smell of tung oil when rubbed on ash gunwales, who keeps its bottom out of the noonday sun, and puts it away under cover. These are the canoeists who make their own paddles, decorating them with motifs that derive from ancient canoe culture, and whether traveling in plastic or canvas canoes load them in the water, not on the beach. Their canoes will be left overturned on the ground the way that others have left theirs, but look carefully. These canoeists have propped the bow and stern of the overturned canoe so that it rests on a piece of wood, not earth or stone.

They and their canoes grow old together gracefully. One owner I know had radiation treatment for a cancer that had spread. For years his response to treatment was as smooth and true as the path his paddle made for him. Around the fire he didn't mention his health, only this trip, the previous one, or one for the future. The leak in the very top of his dome tent responded to the inverted pie pan he put there. When his cancer came back, he didn't complain. He and his boat traveled alone through the salt water of the north, his journal then as inspiring as his campfire stories were earlier. And when he died, his paddles and canoes survived in the hands of those who he knew would take care of them - those who could look at an old canoe that had been loved and while listening to its voice could hear the stories that it held.

Finis

SIXTY YEARS AFTER THAT TRIP in the Boundary Waters, I knelt amidship in a canoe paddled by two of my grown children. We cut outwards from an eddy into the main stream of the Connecticut River, leaning the canoe appropriately to accommodate the change in current. Between my knees was a secure blue box. I lifted the lid and removed the bag within. When we were well out into the current I lifted the bag over the gunwale. I was a bit surprised by its weight. I loosened the bag's neck and the ashes of Jean, my wife, my favorite bow paddler, flowed out into the water and vanished downstream.

In the years between my first trip in the Boundary Waters and my sad trip onto the Connecticut River I had seen lots of paddles and lots of water. Only with Jean's illness had I observed that droplets of water falling from my paddle blade gave birth to beads that spun across the water, dancing for a moment before rejoining their source. For all of time drops of falling water have released offspring that can bounce on the surface of still water, but before this I had not noticed them. What one chooses to see changes during life and this choice reflects what one finds important at the moment.

To those of you who care to look carefully at the water falling from a paddle, notice the beads as they roll on the water's surface. The miracle is that they last as long as they do.

PADDLE BEADS

In the light of dawn or eve
        on water flat
They fall from the moving blade
        and they linger
Roll a moment. A dance
        onto the dark,
A flash of noon
        light in the past.
And then they go;
                water again.

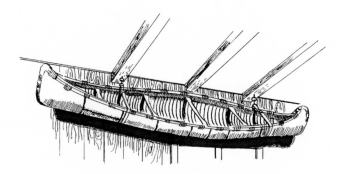

Acknowledgements

I NEVER TOLD YOU WHAT HAPPENED after Engle delivered us to Crane Lake. He unpacked the young campers from his Ford and turned us over to Carter, our Boundary Waters and Quetico guide. With Carter and another counselor we paddled north, entering Canada and Ontario's Quetico Provincial Park. Several days later we left the Namakan River and followed the reed-shrouded meandering channel that would take us into Wisa Lake. As the reeds gave way and the lake spread before us we saw that we were not alone. A black bear swam on a path that intersected ours. As we approached the bear Carter suggested that if we were able to grab the bear's front feet and put them on our gunwale, that it "couldn't do a thing."

The bear, its freedom assured by our vision of the mayhem Carter's plan would cause, swam ashore, scrambled up the beach, and disappeared in the brush as we paddled away.

Carter, a young fellow, too young to be drafted during those World War II years, taught us how to live in the outdoors. In doing so he shared his love and knowledge of the lakes and rivers as we traveled this remote area. With canoe stories, advice about our paddle strokes, and an occasional prick of a self-important balloon he turned a novice group of paddlers into a team that made the trip efficient, safe, and fun.

We left Wisa Lake behind and paddled on. That night was difficult. We had pitched our tent at the only available campsite, a rough rock ledge protruding from the mud-lined shore on a leech-filled lake. Our thin kapok-filled sleeping bags did little to pad our stone bed. Foam pads would be invented twenty years later. Once we were inside the tent, Carter, standing outside, tied the flaps shut and inserted a sprayer through the crack. He pumped it a few times and as the insecticide mist settled, the mosquitoes dropped around us. He then retreated to his mosquito-net protected jungle hammock that swayed between two trees. As we were drifting off to sleep, someone repeated, "Couldn't do a thing!" There were chuckles and then sleep.

The outrageous suggestion that Carter made to us that day was an early example of the humor I have since found widespread in the canoeing world. For me nothing is more pleasurable than to be in the company of canoeists who are telling their stories. Throughout my life the enthusiasm and good spirits I have found amongst paddlers have sustained me and provided comfort when needed.

It is not possible in this space to give credit to all who have contributed to this book, but I must give special recognition to Bert Dodson who illustrated it. My visits with Bert during which we discussed the project were delightful and his insights most helpful. I need also to credit my companions on some of the trips I have mentioned. Chet Harvey and Katherine Armstrong, Jeff and Reed Asher, Bruce Lindwall and Laurie Gullion, Alv Elvestad and Linda Jones have all experienced the threat of our out-of-control canoe corrupting their carefully planned route through white water. When I view the memorial to Barbara Cushwa on Vermont's West River, I think of her rules that served to keep her and those with whom she paddled safe. Ralph Baierlein has taught me more about trip leadership than he will acknowledge. Nor should I forget Pat Beaudry whom we met for the first time when our canoe wrapped on top of hers.

After Jean's passing in 2005, new rivers and friends offered welcome solace. And now my recent bride, Helen Whyte, following a courtship that included Class III rapids, has assumed the bow seat. Last summer we paddled the salt water of Dildo Run in Newfoundland. (It is near Virgin Arm.) We can laugh together at where our boat has taken us.

The members of the Berkshire and New Hampshire Appalachian Mountain Club Canoe Chapters and the Minnesota Rapid Riders have assisted greatly in my education, as has Cliff Jacobson who long ago encouraged me to write about canoeing. I thank Bob Kimber, whose *A Canoeist's Sketchbook*, suggested a format for my book. I'm indebted to Elizabeth Kolbert's *New Yorker* articles about global warming for a portion of the piece on Perpetuity. Ed Gray has cut through opaque prose, straightened crooked syntax and has provided other immeasurable help. Dave Leith, Ed Horton, Helen Whyte and Joe Medlicott have offered advice and I have most gratefully accepted it concerning portions of the manuscript. Segments of two of these pieces have appeared in the Dartmouth Medical School Alumni Notes. A version of the Coppermine piece is found in *Wrap Around*, the New Hampshire Appalachian Mountain Club Canoe Chapter Newsletter.

About the Author

O. ROSS MCINTYRE graduated from Dartmouth College in 1953 and Harvard Medical School in 1957. After serving in Pakistan for the U.S. Public Health Service, he joined the faculty of Dartmouth Medical School in 1964. He retired in 1998, having served as Director of the Norris Cotton Cancer Center at the Dartmouth-Hitchcock Medical Center and as Chairman of the Cancer and Leukemia Group B.

An avid canoeist since boyhood, Ross and his wife of 48 years, the late Jean Geary McIntyre, spent every chance they could deep in the North American wilderness, paddling and camping for weeks at a time, returning afterward to the riverfront New Hampshire farm where he and Jean raised their three children, Jeanie, Ross, and Elizabeth.

CPSIA information can be obtained at www.ICGtesting.com
Printed in the USA
269639BV00001B/55/P